Functional Skills

English

Entry Level 3

This CGP book covers everything you'll need for success in Entry Level 3 Functional Skills English, whichever exam board you're studying.

Every topic is explained with clear, concise notes — and there's a huge range of practice questions and test-style tasks (with detailed answers) to help you make sure you're fully prepared for the final tests.

Since 1995, CGP has helped millions of students do well in their tests and exams. Our books cover dozens of subjects for all ages — at the best prices you'll find anywhere!

Study & Test Practice

Contents

Section 3 — Different Types of Writing

Section 4 — Writing Sentences

Section 5 — Using Correct Spelling

Section 6 — Advice for the Writing Test

Writing Test Practice

Published by CGP

Editors:
Lucy Loveluck
Anthony Muller
Sabrina Robinson
Jo Sharrock
Rebecca Tate

With thanks to Luke von Kotze, Peter Allen, Helen Lawton, David Norden and Susan Blanch for proofreading and reviewing.
With thanks to Laura Collar for the copyright research.

Acknowledgements:
With thanks to iStockphoto.com for permission to reproduce the photograph on page 26.

ISBN: 978 1 78294 631 1

Printed by Elanders Ltd, Newcastle upon Tyne.
Clipart from Corel®

What is Functional English?

Functional Skills are a set of qualifications

1) They are designed to give you the **skills** you need in **everyday life**.
2) There are **three** Functional Skills **subjects** — **English**, **Maths** and **ICT**.
3) You may have to sit **tests** in **one**, **two** or all **three** of these subjects.
4) Each subject has **five levels** — **Entry Level 1-3**, **Level 1** and **Level 2**.

This book is for Functional English

1) There are **three** parts to English — **speaking and listening**, **reading** and **writing**.
2) To get a Functional Skills English qualification, you need to **pass all three parts**.
3) This book covers the **reading** and **writing** parts of **Functional English Entry Level 3**.

Check with your teacher which exam board you're sitting — each board assesses students slightly differently.

Entry Level 3 is tested in controlled assessments

For more about controlled assessments check the glossary.

1) You will need to take three **controlled assessments** in class.
2) They will test you on speaking and listening, reading and writing **separately**.

Reading

- You have to **read texts** and **answer questions** on them.
- Some questions might be **multiple choice** (you choose the correct answer).
- Some questions might ask you to **write** your **answer**.
- You **don't** have to write in **full sentences**.
- You **won't** lose marks if you make **spelling** or **grammar mistakes**.

Writing

- You have to do **two tasks**.
- You **will lose marks** if your spelling, grammar and punctuation are **wrong**.

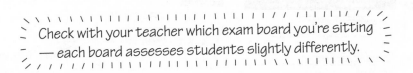

How to Use this Book

This book summarises everything you need to know

1) This book is designed to help you **go over** what you are already learning in class.
2) Use it along with any **notes** and **resources** your teacher has given you.
3) You can work through this book from **start** to **finish**...
4) ... or you can just **pick the topics** that you're **not sure** about.

Use this book to revise and test yourself

1) This book is split into **two parts** — **reading** and **writing**.
2) The topics in each part are usually **spread over two pages**.

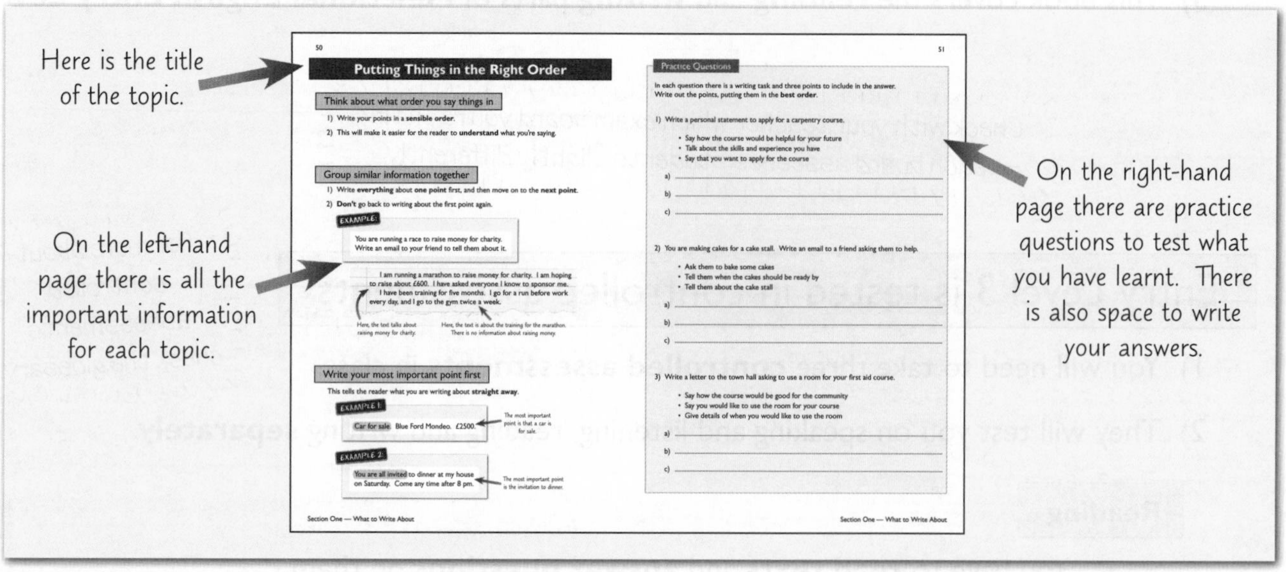
Here is the title of the topic.
On the left-hand page there is all the important information for each topic.
On the right-hand page there are practice questions to test what you have learnt. There is also space to write your answers.
Putting Things in the Right Order
Practice Questions

There are answers to all the practice questions and the test-style practice exercises at the end of each part of the book.

There's lots of test-style practice

1) There are **test-style practice exercises** at the **end** of each part of the book.
2) These exercises are based on **actual Functional Skills assessments.**
3) This means that the questions are **similar** to the ones you'll be asked in the **real tests**.
4) The **reading tests** have a **mix** of **question types** with **space** to write your answers.
5) The **writing tests** have space for a **plan**, but you'll need **extra paper** for your **full answer**.

Using a Dictionary

You can use a dictionary in the test

1) You can use a dictionary to look up the **meaning** of a tricky word.

2) Or you can look up a word to check its **spelling**.

Here's the word you're looking up.

This is one meaning of the word.

simple adj **1** easy to understand or do **2** plain

This is another meaning.

Practise using a dictionary before the test

1) The words in a **dictionary** are listed in **alphabetical order**.

2) This means all the words starting with '**a**' are **grouped together** first, then all the words starting with '**b**', and so on.

3) Words that start with the **same letter** are listed in the order of their **second letter**. For example, '**race**' comes **before** '**rush**'.

4) When you're looking for a word, check the words in **bold** at the **top** of **each page**.

5) These words help you work out which **page** you need to **turn to**.

This tells you that all the words between 'rush' and 'rustle' are covered on this page.

If you want a word that comes before 'rush', turn to an earlier page. If you want a word that comes after 'rustle', turn to a later page.

984 rush | rustle

rush *vb* **1** to hurry

This is the page number of the dictionary.

The first three letters of these words are the same. To put them in order, look at the fourth letter. 'h' comes before 't', so 'rush' comes before 'rustle'.

Don't use a dictionary all the time

1) Dictionaries can be **helpful**, but **don't** use them **too often**.

2) Looking up **lots** of words will **slow you down** in the test...

3) ...so try to **learn** the **spelling** of **tricky** words **before the test**.

If there's a word you don't recognise in this book, use a dictionary to look it up. It's a good way of practising.

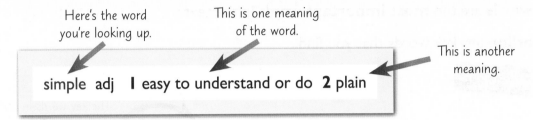

Picking Out the Main Point

The main point of a text is what it is about

1) You **don't** need to read **all** of a text to find the **main point**.
2) Move your eyes **quickly** over the text, looking for **key words**.
3) **Key words** are the **most important** words in the text.
4) **Underline** any key words that you find.

EXAMPLE 1:

Not much is known about the history of Stonehenge. Nobody knows when it was built, but most historians think it must have been between 3000 and 2000 BC.

The key words in the text are underlined. They tell you that the text is about the history of Stonehenge.

EXAMPLE 2:

Taking regular exercise helps to keep you healthy. It reduces your risk of heart disease and diabetes.

The key words tell you that the text is about why exercise is good for you.

The most important point usually comes first

1) Some texts are divided into **paragraphs**. Paragraphs are **groups** of sentences.
2) The **main point** of a text is often in the **first paragraph**.

EXAMPLE:

Send

From: gavin.kelley@web.co.uk
To: j.harrick@nth.com
Subject: Theatre trip

Hi Jonathan,

I'd like to go to the theatre for my birthday next Wednesday. I was wondering if you wanted to come too?

The play I want to see is called 'Men and Boys'. It's a drama set in World War Two. The tickets are £20 each. I can buy them for us.

The invitation to go to the theatre is the most important point. It is in the first paragraph.

The second paragraph gives extra details.

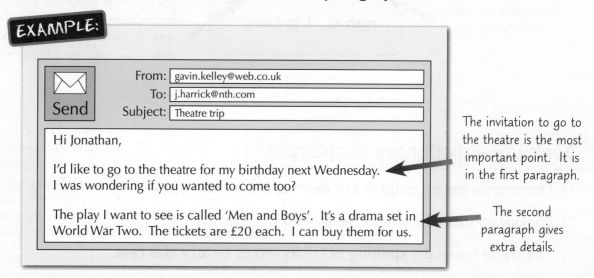

Practice Questions

Read each text below and then answer the question next to it. Circle your answer.

Blue River

Members-only swimming club

Blue River is an exclusive swimming club in Tunaley. Our facilities include:

- A 50-metre swimming pool
- A bubble pool and steam room
- Sports massage

Open 7 am to 10 pm every day.

1) This text is about:

a) A swimming club

b) Sports massage

c) Swimming lessons

d) Tunaley

GET ON YOUR BIKE

Cycling is a great way to get around. The best things about cycling are:

- It's free
- It's good for the environment
- It's good exercise

There are lots of ways to get involved in cycling. Look out for a local cycling club in your town or go out with a friend. Don't forget to wear a helmet!

2) This text:

a) Tells you about cycling helmets

b) Persuades you to do more exercise

c) Tells you about cycling

d) Advertises a cycling club

Cleaner Wanted

Family looking for an experienced cleaner for a large 5-bedroom house in West Tranby. Duties to include:

- General household cleaning
- Ironing
- Laundry

4 hours per week. Pay from £9 an hour depending on experience. References required.
Please contact Mrs Anita Rao on **0141 655 8767**.

3) This text:

a) Tells you about Anita Rao

b) Advertises a cleaning job

c) Advertises a house for sale

d) Tells you about West Tranby

iNTER-COFFEE

George Street, Handelby

We have 12 computers with high-speed internet, plus free Wi-Fi for all our customers.

Coffee, cake and snacks served all day.

Open 8 am to 11 pm Monday to Saturday.

4) This text is about:

a) The internet

b) George Street

c) A restaurant

d) An internet café

Using Key Words to Find Information

Look for key words in the question and the text

1) You **don't** have to read the **whole text** to find a piece of information.
2) Underline the **key words** in the **question**.
3) Quickly **read** through the text, looking for these **key words**.
4) When you find one, read the rest of the sentence **carefully** to find the answer.

See p.4 for more on key words.

EXAMPLE:

1) How often should you collect your mail?

This question is about collecting your mail. Look for the word 'collect' in the text.

> **Using a Post Office (PO) box**
>
> Having your mail sent to a PO box lets you keep the address of your company private.
>
> If you have a PO box you must collect your mail once a month. The Post Office can deliver mail from PO boxes for an extra fee.

The word 'collect' is here. Read the rest of the sentence to find the answer.

The answer is 'once a month'.

Think about what the question means

The key words in the **question** might not be **exactly** the same as the words in the **text**.

EXAMPLE:

1) Give **one** example of a subject you can try at the open day.

This question is asking about subjects.

> **Mid-Valley Language School**
>
> Mid-Valley Language School is having an open day on Thursday 14th May. Come and have a free taster session.
> We have lots of classes on offer:
>
> French German Spanish Arabic Mandarin

'Classes' means the same as subjects.

There are five options that answer the question. Choose one of them.

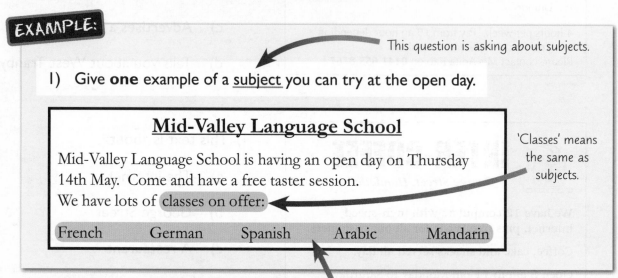

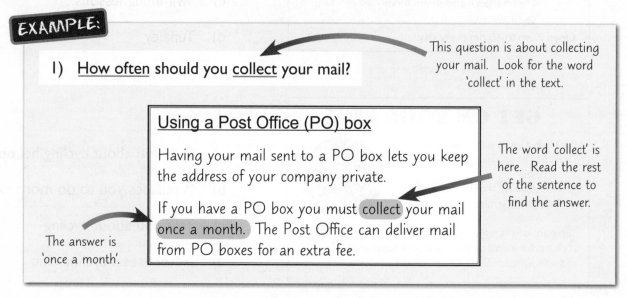

Practice Questions

Read the text below and then answer the questions underneath.

Upper Tarnford to get bypass

Traffic has been increasing in Upper Tarnford over the last 5 years. Now the council have decided to build a bypass around the town. The council hope a bypass will reduce traffic problems in the area.

Upper Tarnford town centre is often full of cars and lorries. The roads are particularly busy at rush hour. Most of the traffic is passing through from Kellingworth to Lower Tarnford. The new bypass would mean people could drive past Upper Tarnford rather than through it.

Some people are worried that the bypass will affect the environment. It will cut through a large part of Pavey Wood. This area is very popular with birdwatchers because it is home to a rare type of sparrow.

Construction of the bypass is due to begin in September. It will take 6 months to complete.

What do you think about the bypass? Have your say. Visit our website: www.tarnfordgazette.co.uk/bypass.

1) How long has the traffic been increasing in Upper Tarnford? Circle your answer.

a) The last 3 years

b) The last 5 years

c) Since September

d) The last 6 months

2) Who has decided to build the bypass? Circle your answer.

a) Local people

b) Car drivers

c) The council

d) Birdwatchers

3) When will the building of the bypass start?

....

4) When is the traffic in Upper Tarnford at its worst?

....

5) You want to give your opinion about the bypass. What should you do?

....

....

Using Layout to Find Information

Use subheadings to help you find information

1) **Subheadings** are titles in the text that tell you what each **section** is **about**.
2) Look for **subheadings** that **match** the information you need.
3) **Read** the **text** under that **subheading**. The **answer** will probably be there.

EXAMPLE:

1) Name **two** activities you can do in Hereford.

Look for subheadings with the word 'activities'.

Visit Hereford

When to go:

Try to avoid school holidays when the city gets very busy.

Where to stay:

There are several hotels in the city itself, or many pleasant B&Bs in the area.

Activities:

You could visit the cathedral, which is open daily. You could also cross the Old Wye Bridge or take a tour of the Town Hall.

Outside the City:

- Hay-on-Wye
- West Midlands Safari Park

The subheading tells you that this section is about activities. Check here first.

There are three options that answer the question. Choose two of them.

Some questions ask which section a piece of information is in

1) **Find** the piece of information you are being asked about.
2) Look at the **subheading** above it. This is the answer.

EXAMPLE:

1) You want to find out what to take with you if you have to leave your home during a flood. What section is this information in?

Flood Awareness

Flood warnings:

Flood warnings are given during periods of heavy rain. Flood warnings can be green, amber or red. A red warning is the worst. It means flooding is very likely.

Evacuation:

In rare cases people have to be evacuated during a flood. If you have to leave your home, you should take food, water, warm clothes and a mobile phone with you.

This is the information you are looking for.

The subheading above this information is 'Evacuation'. This is the answer.

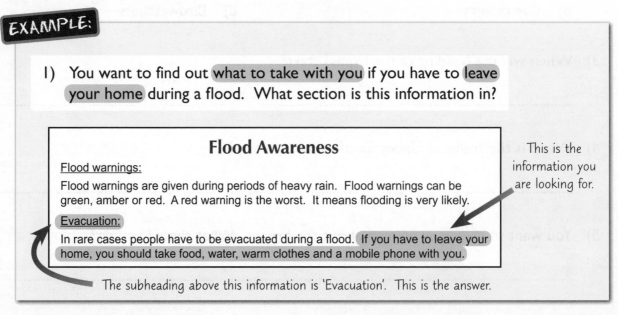

Practice Questions

Read the text below and then answer the questions underneath.

FIRST AID TRAINING — 20th SEPTEMBER

The training will cover:

Heart attacks
Choking
Bleeding
Broken bones
Burns

How we teach:

The training is given by Joe Thandie. Joe has been a first aider for 33 years. He will show the group each skill. Then you will be given time to practise on each other. Role play is an important way of teaching first aid, so you need to be prepared to take part.

On the day:

The course begins at 9 am. Please get there early. The day will be taught in five sessions. Each session will last one hour. There will be coffee breaks in between. These will give you a chance to talk to Joe and the other people on the course.

The day will finish with a short test. You will be asked to act out a situation in front of the group. If you pass, you will be given a certificate which is valid for two years.

How to book:

Telephone 0181 564 2398 and speak to Janine Newton. The course costs £50.

1) Give **one** thing that is covered in the training.

....

2) You want to find out what time the course starts. What section is this information in?

....

3) Who is teaching the first aid course?

....

4) Which section of the text should you look in to find out how much the course costs?

....

5) How many sessions are there on the day? Circle your answer.

a) Thirty-three
c) Nine
b) Five
d) One

6) You want to book a place on the course. What should you do?

....

....

Using Layout to Find Information

Bullet points can help you find information

They **separate** information so it is **easier** to **read**.

EXAMPLE:

1) Give **two** ways of contacting Tiger Jewels.

If you have a complaint, please contact us by:

- Emailing us at complaints@tigerjewels.com
- Telephoning us on 01222 333 444

These are the two answers to the question. The bullet points make them easier to spot.

Words might be written in bold or in capital letters

This makes **important** information **stand out**.

EXAMPLE:

Helmets and protective clothing MUST be worn at all times when inside the paintballing arena. **Do not** remove your helmet until you have left the arena.

This is important. It is in capital letters so it stands out.

This is in bold so you notice it when you are reading the sentence.

Sometimes the answer will be in a table

Use the **column headings** to help you find the information.

EXAMPLE:

1) Who is working on the till on Saturday?

Columns go down the table.

Rows go across the table.

Visitor Centre Staff Rota

Day	Supervisor	Helpdesk	Café	Till
Monday	Marcus	Heather	Luka	Jill
Wednesday	Ravi	Jill	Luka	Susannah
Saturday	Ravi	Luka	Susannah	Jill

The column headings show you where to find each bit of information.

Go to the row for Saturday. Look along this row until you get to the column for the till. The answer is 'Jill'.

Practice Questions

Read the text below and then answer the questions underneath.

Wallsea Birdwatching Cruises

"A wonderful experience! We saw so many different birds, and our children loved it."

A Wallsea Birdwatching Cruise is a perfect family day out. Children will enjoy the **beautiful coastline** and **interesting wildlife**. Birds that are often seen include:

- Puffins
- Arctic terns
- Gannets
- Fulmars
- Sea eagles
- Pacific gulls

Cruises run throughout the summer. See table for times.

Months	Daily departure times			
June		11.30 am	1.30 pm	
July	10.00 am	11.30 am	3.00 pm	
August	10.00 am	12.00 pm	2.00 pm	4.00 pm

ALL PASSENGERS MUST WEAR LIFE JACKETS

1) Name **one** type of bird you could see on a Wallsea Birdwatching Cruise.

....

2) Give **two** things children will enjoy on a Wallsea Birdwatching Cruise.

1 ....

2 ....

3) You want to go on a cruise in the afternoon on the 7th June.
What time could you go? Circle your answer.

a) 10.00 am

b) 11.30 am

c) 1.30 pm

d) 4.00 pm

4) What do passengers have to wear on the boat?

....

5) Which month has tours at 4.00 pm?

....

Different Types of Question

You might have to choose the right answer from a list

1) For some questions you will be given a **right** answer and some **wrong** ones.
2) Look at each option **carefully**.
3) **Rule out** the options that are **definitely wrong** until you are left with the **right answer**.

EXAMPLE:

Soup is an easy and healthy dish to cook. Just take your favourite vegetables (for example, carrots, potatoes or broccoli) and boil them in water until they are soft. Then mash or blend them to make a soup. Add water, salt and pepper.

1) How long should you boil the vegetables for?

a) ~~Until they are mashed~~

b) ~~For 15 minutes~~

c) ~~For 10 minutes~~

d) Until they are soft

The text only mentions mashing the vegetables after they are boiled. This is not the right answer.

The text does not say how many minutes to boil them for. Both of these are wrong.

This is the right answer. The text says 'boil them until they are soft'.

You might have to write down your own answer

1) **Read** the question **carefully** and work out what information it is asking for.
2) **Find** that information in the text and **write** it in the space you are given.

EXAMPLE:

The car was travelling along the road. A cyclist rode out from a driveway in front of it. He was wearing a green helmet and he had a red bike. The car turned off the road to avoid the cyclist. It hit a tree and was damaged. The cyclist rode off.

The question asks you about the colour of the bike. Look in the text for the answer.

1) What colour was the cyclist's bike?

......red......

The text says the bike was 'red'.

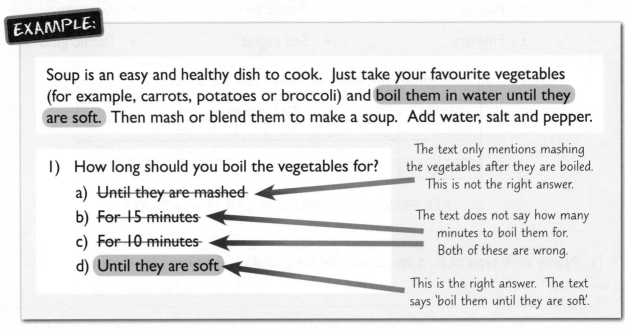

Practice Questions

Read the text below and then answer the questions underneath.

CHARITY TALENT SHOW

To raise funds for *St Crispin's Hospice*

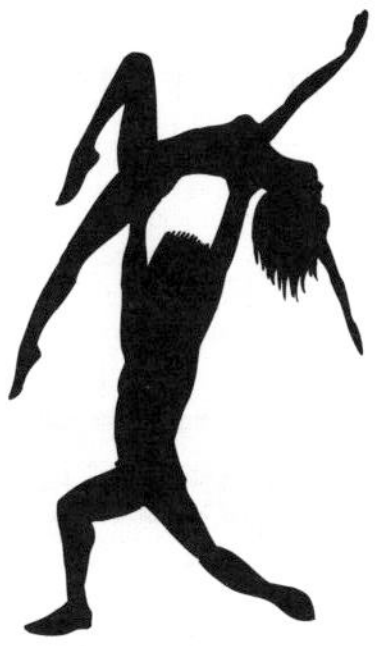

- Have you got a talent you would like to share?
  We are looking for 25 performers for our talent show.
- Dancers, singers, magicians.
  We want anyone with a special talent.
- The show will take place at the Mile Park Hotel.
  There will be an audience of 300 people.
- The winner will receive £50 of theatre vouchers.
  They will also perform on Go East Television's Breakfast News.

Auditions on Thursday 11th November, 10 am to 4 pm at Firely End Town Hall.

Call Mark on 06652 765791 for more information.

1) How many people will watch the talent show? Circle your answer.

a) 100   c) 50

b) 25   d) 300

2) What does the winner receive? Circle your answer.

a) £50 of theatre vouchers   c) A dance lesson

b) Their picture will go in the paper   d) A meal at Mile Park Hotel

3) What charity is the talent show raising money for?

....

4) You want more information about the talent show. What should you do?

....

5) What date will the auditions be held on?

....

Looking Up Tricky Words

Look up words you don't understand

1) The texts in the reading test might contain words you **don't understand**.
2) You can use your **dictionary** to find out what these words mean.
3) Words in the dictionary are organised in **alphabetical** order.

There is more about how to use a dictionary on p. 3.

Some questions might ask you to use a dictionary

1) You might get a question that asks you to look up a **word**.
2) Use a **dictionary** for these questions, even if you think you **know** what the word means.
3) Some dictionaries give **more than one** meaning for each word. Only write down **one**.

EXAMPLE:

This is the word you need to look up.

1) Use a dictionary look up the word '**oppose**'. Write down what it means.

Here is the dictionary entry for 'oppose'.

You only need to write down one of these meanings.

oppose *vb* **1** to be in conflict with **2** to be resistant to

Only look up words when you really need to

1) Looking up lots of words will **slow** you down in the test.
2) Try to **work out** what a word means by looking at the rest of the **sentence**.

EXAMPLE:

'Refer' is a difficult word. Look at the rest of the sentence to work out what it means.

Follow the instructions carefully. If you are unsure about anything, refer back to the user's manual.

The sentence is about looking at a user's manual. 'Refer' must mean 'look'.

Practice Questions

1) Read the text and use a dictionary to answer the questions below.

> http://www.harrietbrowningfanclub.com
>
> **Harriet Browning Fan Club** Search:
>
> A note to our readers
>
> This is not an official fan website. None of the opinions given on this site represent the opinions of the author Harriet Browning. Any information about Harriet Browning or her books may not be accurate. Contact info@harrietbrowningfanclub.com to find out more.

a) Use a dictionary to look up the word '**official**'. Write down what it means.

b) Use a dictionary to look up the word '**represent**'. Write down what it means.

c) Use a dictionary to look up the word '**accurate**'. Write down what it means.

2) Use a dictionary to look up the word '**prohibit**'. Write down what it means.

3) Use a dictionary to look up the word '**specialist**'. Write down what it means.

4) Use a dictionary to look up the word '**supervise**'. Write down what it means.

During the Reading Test

Read the text carefully

1) Read the **whole text** before you answer the questions.
2) Make sure you understand **what the text is about**.
3) **Look up** tricky words if you need to.

EXAMPLE:

This text is a job advert for a receptionist.

You could use your dictionary to look up words like 'exceptional'.

We are a law firm looking for a receptionist to join our Birmingham office. You must have previous experience and exceptional communication skills. To apply please send a CV to the address below.

Read the question carefully

1) Make sure you understand **what the question is asking** before you answer it.
2) Look **back at the text** to check your answer before you write it down.

EXAMPLE:

1) What city would the receptionist be working in?

This question is asking for the name of a city. Look back at the text to check where the receptionist job is. The answer is 'Birmingham'.

Follow the instructions

1) The question always tells you **what you need to do**.
2) **Underline** the **important words** to make it easier to follow the instructions.

EXAMPLE:

1) List <u>two things</u> somebody applying for this job must have.

You need to write two different things. These are 'previous experience' and 'exceptional communication skills'.

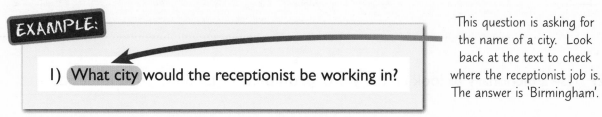

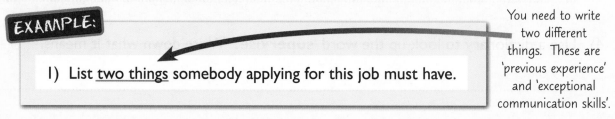

During the Reading Test

Answer as many questions as you can

1) If you can't do a question, **leave it** and **move on** to the next one.
2) You can **come back** to the questions you have left if you have time at the end.
3) If you finish early, **check your answers**.
4) Read the questions again. Make sure what you have written **answers** the question.

Don't worry too much about spelling

1) **Don't worry** if you are not sure how to spell a word.
2) Your spelling **will not** be marked in the reading test.
3) You just need to make sure that what you write can be **understood**.
4) Make sure your handwriting is **clear**.

You don't need to write in full sentences

1) In the reading test you **will not** get marks for writing in **full sentences**.
2) Just write enough to **answer the question**.

EXAMPLE:

The council have started a new rubbish-collection scheme. All houses in the area have been given a new bin and recycling boxes. The recycling is collected every week and the rubbish is collected every other week. The scheme has been running for five weeks. It is very popular so far.

1) How long has the rubbish-collection scheme been running for?

........................five weeks........................

You can just write one or two words for your answer. You don't need to write a sentence.

Source A — Swimming Club

Read **Source A** and answer the questions that follow. You have 20 minutes to do this exercise.

For multiple-choice questions, circle the letter you have chosen.
For standard answer questions, write your answer in the space provided.
You do not have to write in full sentences. You may use a dictionary.

You would like to do more swimming. You pick up this leaflet in your leisure centre.

SPARK BRIDGE SWIMMING CLUB

We are looking for swimmers who are dedicated, positive and friendly to join our club at Spark Bridge swimming pool.

We have three levels of swimming sessions:

Level	Days	Times
Beginner	Monday, Friday	6pm to 7pm
Intermediate	Tuesday, Thursday	6pm to 7pm
Advanced	Wednesday, Friday	7pm to 8pm

Our Team

Kathy, Mick and Paul are all professional coaches who can help you swim faster, and learn new techniques. The coaches will be at the swimming pool during every session, so you will get plenty of support and advice.

For extra safety, two of our fully-trained lifeguards are also constantly watching the swimming pool.

Joining the Club

Everyone is welcome to come along to a FREE taster session every Friday at 6pm. Monthly membership costs just £35. See the pool reception for more details.

For more information contact Jim Davies:

Telephone - 07633526347 Email - swim@sparkbridge.co.uk

1) Where is the swimming club held?

....

(1 mark)

2) What kind of swimmers is the club looking for? Give **three** qualities from Source A.

a) ....

b) ....

c) ....

(3 marks)

3) When do intermediate sessions take place?

a) Tuesday and Wednesday

b) Monday and Thursday

c) Tuesday and Thursday

d) Monday and Friday

(1 mark)

4) Who will help you to swim faster if you join the club?

a) Lifeguards

b) Other club members

c) Swimming coaches

d) Jim Davies

(1 mark)

5) Which section of Source A gives you information about taster sessions?

....

(1 mark)

6) According to the text, who should you contact for more information?

....

(1 mark)

Source B — Charity Day

Read **Source B** and answer the questions that follow. You have 20 minutes to do this exercise.

For multiple-choice questions, circle the letter you have chosen.
For standard answer questions, write your answer in the space provided.
You do not have to write in full sentences. You may use a dictionary.

You receive this email while at work.

Send

From: jill.m@jzm_electronics.co.uk
To: allstaff_jzm
Subject: Charity Day

Dear All,

This year's charity day is just around the corner. It will take place on Friday 14th July. We will be holding a number of activities to raise money for the village school.

For £2 you can wear your own clothes instead of your uniform. Simply pay the money to your team leader and you can wear your jeans.

Raffle tickets will be on sale throughout the week, starting from Monday 10th July. Many local shops and restaurants have already donated prizes and vouchers. The winning tickets will be chosen on Friday afternoon.

We will have a cake stall in the canteen from 12 pm, which will be full of delicious homemade goodies.

Pupils from Grangeville Primary School will be visiting the office between 3 pm and 5 pm to offer a carwash service. Remember to bring plenty of spare change.

If anyone would like to bake a cake or donate a raffle prize please contact me by replying to this email or calling 02276 623445.

Kind Regards,

Jill Martin
HR Assistant

JZM Electronics

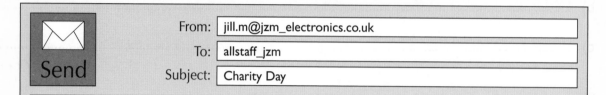

1) According to Source B, what is the money being raised for?

a) Local shops

b) The village school

c) The village car wash

d) The raffle

(1 mark)

2) What date will the charity day be held on?

....

(1 mark)

3) How much will it cost to wear jeans for the day?

....

(1 mark)

4) According to Source B, give **two** things that local businesses have donated.

a) ....

b) ....

(2 marks)

5) What charity event will be held in the canteen?

....

(1 mark)

6) Give **two** reasons why people should contact Jill Martin.

a) ....

b) ....

(2 marks)

Source C — Clothing Adjustments

Read **Source C** and answer the questions that follow. You have 20 minutes to do this exercise.

For multiple-choice questions, circle the letter you have chosen.
For standard answer questions, write your answer in the space provided.
You do not have to write in full sentences. You may use a dictionary.

Your new trousers are too long. You find this advert about a clothes adjustments shop.

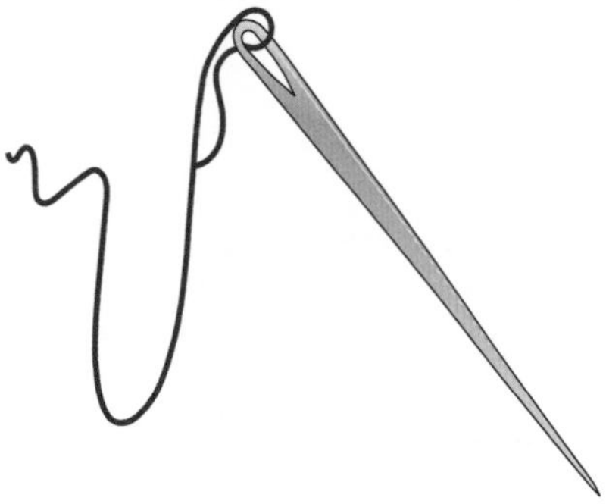

The Neat Needle

Clothes Repairs and Adjustments

Find us next to the market, on Bridge Street.

The Neat Needle first opened in 1988, when Sara Davies decided to turn her sewing hobby into a successful business.

Since then, Sara has trained three part-time assistants. Together they adjust a huge range of items every day. Their highly-skilled sewing service and good value for money make The Neat Needle the best choice when you need your clothes adjusted.

Price List

Repairing rips— £10.00
Shortening trousers — £10.00
Shortening skirts — £12.00
Adjusting shirt sleeves — £9.00
Zip replacement — £11.00

- Have your items ready the same day for £1 extra. Just bring them in before 3 pm.
- Try our new overnight ironing service. Ask in store for more information.
- Spend over £20 and receive a £5 voucher.

1) Find the word '**adjust**' in your dictionary and write down its meaning.

....

....

(1 mark)

2) According to Source C, when did The Neat Needle first open?

....

(1 mark)

3) According to Source C, give **two** reasons why customers should choose The Neat Needle.

a) ....

....

b) ....

....

(2 marks)

4) How much would it cost to get some trousers shortened?

....

(1 mark)

5) You want your clothes to be ready the same day. You have to take them to the shop before:

a) 12 pm

c) 10 am

b) 2 pm

d) 3 pm

(1 mark)

6) How much do you have to spend to get a £5 voucher?

....

(1 mark)

7) What is the new overnight service?

a) Ironing

c) Curtain making

b) Dry cleaning

d) Delivery

(1 mark)

Source D — Lunch Menu

Read **Source D** and answer the questions that follow. You have 20 minutes to do this exercise.

For multiple-choice questions, circle the letter you have chosen.
For standard answer questions, write your answer in the space provided.
You do not have to write in full sentences. You may use a dictionary.

You are having lunch at a restaurant. Here is the menu.

SUNDAY LUNCH AT THE RAM & GOAT

We would like to welcome you to the Ram and Goat, one of the best restaurants in Cumbria. We are located in the Eden Valley and have served food for 75 years. Our warm atmosphere brings customers back again and again.

We only use ingredients from the local area, and our dishes are always homemade and beautifully presented.

STARTERS

Prawn cocktail

Tomato and basil soup served with a white or brown bread roll

MAIN COURSES

Roast beef served with roast potatoes and vegetables

Grilled salmon with green salad and a peppercorn sauce

Spinach, cheese and potato bake

DESSERTS

Rich chocolate fudge cake

Summer fruits cheesecake

Children's Menu — £9

Includes any main course, any dessert and a soft drink. Exactly the same as our adult dishes but in child-sized portions.

Main course — £9
2 courses — £13
3 courses — £16

1) According to Source D, why do customers return to the Ram and Goat?

....

(1 mark)

2) Where does the restaurant get its ingredients from?

....

(1 mark)

3) Name **two** things you can have as a starter.

a) ....

b) ....

(2 marks)

4) Your friend does not like potatoes. Which main course should he choose?

....

....

(1 mark)

5) Name one thing you can have for dessert.

....

(1 mark)

6) How much does it cost for an adult to have a main course and a dessert?

....

(1 mark)

7) Which of these is included in the Children's Menu?

a) A starter

b) Chocolate cake

c) Apple pie

d) Chips

(1 mark)

Source E — Grow Your Own Herbs

Read **Source E** and answer the questions that follow. You have 20 minutes to do this exercise.

For multiple-choice questions, circle the letter you have chosen.
For standard answer questions, write your answer in the space provided.
You do not have to write in full sentences. You may use a dictionary.

You would like to grow your own herbs. You find this information at the garden centre.

Grow Your Own Herbs

Many people enjoy cooking with herbs. However, buying them in the supermarket can be very expensive. Growing your own is much cheaper and herbs like thyme, basil and parsley are quite easy to grow indoors.

Your herbs will need plenty of sunlight to help them grow, so make sure you keep your plant pots on a windowsill.

You will need:

- a plant pot
- compost
- seeds

Method

1) Fill your pot with compost until it is about three-quarters full.
2) Sprinkle a thin layer of seeds onto the compost.
3) Place just enough compost on top of your seeds to cover them.
4) Water your seeds and wait for them to grow.

Useful Hints

Make sure you water your herbs regularly.

Check the back of the seed packet to find the best time to plant them.

1) What is the main point of this text?

a) To encourage you to grow vegetables

b) To tell you how to grow herbs

c) To advertise compost

d) To teach you how to cook

(1 mark)

2) According to Source E, where should you keep your plant pots?

....

(1 mark)

3) Name **three** herbs that the text says are easy to grow.

a) ....

b) ....

c) ....

(3 marks)

4) How much compost should you put on top of your seeds?

....

(1 mark)

5) You are planting some herb seeds. According to the text, what should you do first?

a) Water your seeds

b) Sprinkle the seeds into the pot

c) Fill the pot with compost

d) Wash your hands

(1 mark)

6) You want to know the best time to plant your seeds.
Where does the text say you should look?

....

(1 mark)

Source F — Cheaper Train Travel

Read **Source F** and answer the questions that follow. You have 20 minutes to do this exercise.

For multiple-choice questions, circle the letter you have chosen.
For standard answer questions, write your answer in the space provided.
You do not have to write in full sentences. You may use a dictionary.

You would like to save some money on train tickets. You find this leaflet at the station.

Make your Money go Further

Trains are a popular way to travel. They are good for the environment and train journeys are often much less stressful than car journeys. However, tickets can be very expensive, which may make you look for other ways to travel.

If you want to continue using trains, try to make sure you get the best value fares. If possible, book your tickets in advance. The price of your ticket will go up as the date of your journey gets closer. It is best to buy your tickets as soon as you know the date of your journey.

If you are ordering your tickets online, always compare the prices on different websites to find the best deal.

Rail card holders can get money off their tickets. There are different rail cards for different groups of people, like young people, families and people over 65. Check with your rail company to see if you can apply for any.

If you make the same journey every day, then buying a weekly or monthly ticket could save you some money.

To find out more, go to the ticket office at your local station.
You could also call our Travel Helpline on 02734 654372.

1) You give this information to a friend. You tell him it will help him to:

a) Find a train timetable

c) Get rid of his stress

b) Save money on train tickets

d) Avoid traffic jams

(1 mark)

2) Give **one** reason from Source F why train travel is popular.

....

....

(1 mark)

3) Why does the text say people might be put off using trains?

a) Tickets are expensive

c) Cars get stuck in traffic

b) Cars are faster

d) You can buy tickets online

(1 mark)

4) Name **two** ways of buying cheaper tickets suggested in the text.

a) ....

....

b) ....

....

(2 marks)

5) Why does the text say you should book your tickets in advance?

....

....

(1 mark)

6) Give **two** ways you can find out more about getting cheaper train tickets.

a) ....

b) ....

(2 marks)

Source G — Moving House

Read **Source G** and answer the questions that follow. You have 20 minutes to do this exercise.

For multiple-choice questions, circle the letter you have chosen.
For standard answer questions, write your answer in the space provided.
You do not have to write in full sentences. You may use a dictionary.

You are about to move house and you read this advert.

MOVE E-Z

Moving house or flat can be very stressful. Here at Move E-Z we provide everything you need to make moving a breeze.

SERVICES INCLUDE:

- **Helping you pack up**
- **Cleaning your old property**
- **Unpacking in your new home**

EXPERIENCED COMPANY

Our staff are careful, friendly and supportive, so there is nothing for you to worry about. You can be sure that all your items will be packed safely and everything will arrive intact. If anything is damaged during the move we will replace it for you as quickly as possible.

We will take on any job, but we specialise in helping elderly people move.

PRICING

To arrange a free inspection of your property, call us on **09800 757578**, or email us at **mail@move_ez.com**. We can provide a quote for any job within two working days. This quote will include all costs, so there will be no nasty surprises.

MOVE E-Z *Making moving E-Z* MOVE E-Z

1) According to Source G, which of these statements is true?

a) The company only helps elderly people
c) Inspections take three working days
b) Quotes include all costs
d) Move E-Z staff are careless

(1 mark)

2) What type of move does Move E-Z say they are best at?

a) Big moves
c) Moves for old people
b) House moves
d) Small moves

(1 mark)

3) According to Source G, what will Move E-Z do if they damage anything?

....

(1 mark)

4) You want to arrange an inspection. Give **two** ways of contacting Move E-Z.

a) ....

b) ....

(2 marks)

5) Find the word '**intact**' in your dictionary and write down its meaning.

....

....

(1 mark)

6) List **two** words used to describe the staff at Move E-Z.

a) ....

b) ....

(2 marks)

Source H — Application Form Advice

Read **Source H** and answer the questions that follow. You have 20 minutes to do this exercise.

For multiple-choice questions, circle the letter you have chosen.
For standard answer questions, write your answer in the space provided.
You do not have to write in full sentences. You may use a dictionary.

You need to fill in an application form. You are looking for advice and you read this webpage.

http://www.certainsuccesscareers.co.uk

Application Forms

Certain Success Careers Advice

Covering Letters | Application Forms | CVs | Interviews

Filling in a job application form can be difficult.
Here is some simple advice to help you.

Basic Checklist

1) Read all the instructions first. Some forms may ask you to use black ink only.
2) Send everything you are asked for. For example, you might be asked to include a photograph of yourself.
3) Answer all of the questions.
4) Make sure you spell everything right, especially the company's name.
5) Get a friend or family member to check your application for you.

Experience and Personal Skills

There are lots of skills you might have, even if you have not worked for a while. You might have developed personal skills outside of work. For example:

- If you play football, you might be very good at teamwork.
- If you have children, you might be good at managing your time.

References

References are statements from other people saying what kind of person you are. You could ask your most recent employer, a teacher or a tutor for a reference. Remember to ask for their permission first.

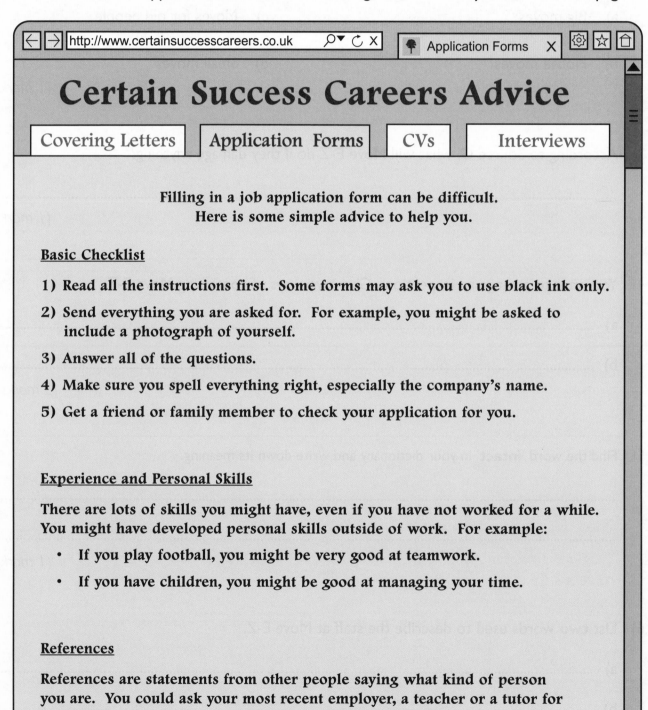

1) What does this web page help you to do?

a) Fill in an application form

b) Find a job

c) Write a reference

d) Write a CV

(1 mark)

2) According to Source H, when you fill in an application form you must:

a) Always write in pencil

b) Include a photo of yourself

c) Never show your application to others

d) Answer all the questions

(1 mark)

3) You are about to fill in a job application form. What does the text say you should do first?

....

....

(1 mark)

4) List **two** personal skills the text says you could have developed outside of work.

a) ....

b) ....

(2 marks)

5) You need a reference for your application. List **three** people that the text suggests you could ask for a reference.

a) ....

b) ....

c) ....

(3 marks)

Source I — Family Day Out

Read **Source I** and answer the questions that follow. You have 20 minutes to do this exercise.

For multiple-choice questions, circle the letter you have chosen.
For standard answer questions, write your answer in the space provided.
You do not have to write in full sentences. You may use a dictionary.

You are on holiday with your family. You find this leaflet in the tourist information centre.

Broadbridge House

Visit Broadbridge House for a wonderful day out with the whole family. Broadbridge House is a large country house in the beautiful Sussex countryside. Admire our stunning ballroom or our award-winning rose garden. Wander through our grounds enjoying the spectacular views.

Facilities

Restaurant serving snacks, light lunches and evening meals

Footpaths around the grounds (accessible to wheelchairs)

Donkey rides for children under 12 years old

Kayak hire on the lake in summer

Family Fun Days

Family fun days are held throughout the summer. There are plenty of activities to keep everyone entertained. You can dress up in historical costumes, or win great prizes in our treasure hunts. We have a variety of games as well as an assault course.

See our website for more details: www.broadbridgehouse.co.uk

1) What is Broadbridge House?

a) A donkey rescue centre

b) A country house

c) A café

d) A museum

(1 mark)

2) What has Broadbridge House won a prize for?

....

(1 mark)

3) Which section of the text has information about the restaurant at Broadbridge House?

....

(1 mark)

4) You would like to hire a kayak. What time of year can you do this?

....

(1 mark)

5) List **three** things from the text that guests could enjoy on a Family Fun Day.

a) ....

b) ....

c) ....

(3 marks)

6) You want more information about Broadbridge House. What should you do?

a) Send them an email

b) Visit the house's help desk

c) Phone them

d) Go to the website

(1 mark)

Source J — Winter Driving

Read **Source J** and answer the questions that follow. You have 20 minutes to do this exercise.

For multiple-choice questions, circle the letter you have chosen.
For standard answer questions, write your answer in the space provided.
You do not have to write in full sentences. You may use a dictionary.

You read this poster at your local garage.

Driving Safely in Winter

In the winter, there is often ice and snow on the roads. This leads to more accidents at this time of year. Follow this advice to stay safe when driving.

Before Driving

- Always check the forecast for weather warnings.
- In very bad weather, try to avoid driving at all.
- Keep a winter survival kit in your car. This should include a blanket, a small shovel, a torch, warm clothes and waterproof boots.
- Remove any snow or ice from your car before driving. You must not have any on your windows, mirrors or lights when you set off.

While Driving

- Go slowly. Accelerate and brake gently. Use the highest gear that you can. These things will help you stay in control of your car on icy roads.
- Leave plenty of space between your car and the vehicle in front. It can take your car ten times longer to stop on icy roads.
- Listen to local news on the radio. This can tell you about bad weather or traffic accidents.
- If you get stuck, call the emergency services.

1) What does this poster do?

a) Advises people on safe winter driving

b) Convinces people to wear warm clothes

c) Encourages people to stay indoors

d) Teaches people to survive in winter

(1 mark)

2) According to Source J, why are there more accidents in the winter?

....

....

(1 mark)

3) List **three** things that the text says you should have in your winter survival kit.

a) ....

b) ....

c) ....

(3 marks)

4) Why should you leave more space between yourself and other cars during bad weather?

a) So you can see them better

b) They might be using a high gear

c) They might be going very slowly

d) It will take you longer to stop

(1 mark)

5) What does the poster say you should do in very bad weather?

....

(1 mark)

6) According to the text, who should you call if you get stuck in snow?

....

(1 mark)

Source K — Job Advert

Read **Source** K and answer the questions that follow. You have 20 minutes to do this exercise.

For multiple-choice questions, circle the letter you have chosen.
For standard answer questions, write your answer in the space provided.
You do not have to write in full sentences. You may use a dictionary.

You are looking for a new job and you see this advert in a newspaper.

Better Health Pharmacy

Better Health Pharmacy is looking for two new members of staff to join our busy pharmacy in the town centre.

Part-Time Pharmacy Assistant

This position is part-time, Monday to Wednesday. You may also work some weekends. Previous experience is not required as full training will be given. The job will include:

- Serving customers at the sales counter and over the telephone.
- Checking stock and stock prices.
- Keeping the shop clean and tidy.
- Helping other staff when needed.

We are looking for a good team member who is friendly to customers and other staff.

Full-Time Store Manager

This position is full-time, Monday to Friday. You must have experience of managing a pharmacy. The role will include:

- Managing a small team of staff.
- Meeting targets set by the area manager.
- Managing the finances of the store.

We are looking for someone confident and hardworking who is a good team leader.

If you would like more information about these jobs, please call Gita on 01739 448670.

1) Where is the pharmacy?

....

(1 mark)

2) What days will the pharmacy assistant work?

a) Monday to Friday

b) Monday to Wednesday

c) Every Saturday

d) Thursday to Sunday

(1 mark)

3) Name **two** tasks the pharmacy assistant job will include.

a) ....

....

b) ....

....

(2 marks)

4) According to the advert, the store manager must:

a) Have a car

b) Have previous experience

c) Live in the town centre

d) Be friendly

(1 mark)

5) According to Source K, list **two** of the qualities that the store manager should have.

a) ....

b) ....

(2 marks)

6) You would like more information about the pharmacy assistant job. What should you do?

....

(1 mark)

Source L — New Parents

Read **Source L** and answer the questions that follow. You have 20 minutes to do this exercise.

For multiple-choice questions, circle the letter you have chosen.
For standard answer questions, write your answer in the space provided.
You do not have to write in full sentences. You may use a dictionary.

You read this leaflet in a hospital waiting room.

New Parents

Being a parent is difficult, especially if it is your first baby. This leaflet will give you a few ideas about how to make things easier.

How can I socialise?

It is hard to stay in touch with friends or meet new people when you have a child with you. Try:

- Looking for local parent groups. These groups are a good opportunity to meet other people with children and to arrange play days. You can usually take your child along too.
- Phoning your local council. Councils usually have details of activities and events for young children, such as library story-time.
- Going to a park. You might be surprised at how many parents you will meet taking their children out for some fresh air.

Where can I get support?

Parenting is hard work. Needing help is not a sign of weakness, so don't be afraid to ask for it. Try:

- Talking to a professional. Your GP and health visitor have lots of experience. They will be able to give you advice on many of the problems that new parents face.
- Talking to your friends and family. They might be able to help you with childcare or offer advice based on their own experiences.

1) According to Source L, which of these statements is true?

a) Parenting is easy if it is your first baby
b) Children can usually go to parent groups
c) Needing help is a sign of weakness
d) The internet is not useful for parents

(1 mark)

2) Find the word '**opportunity**' in your dictionary and write down its meaning.

....

....

(1 mark)

3) List **three** things that new parents can do if they want to socialise more.

a) ....

b) ....

c) ....

(3 marks)

4) You want to know more about library story-time. How could you find this information?

....

....

(1 mark)

5) You want to know where new parents can get help.
Which section of the text gives you information about this?

....

(1 mark)

6) Why does this text suggest new parents should talk to a professional?

a) Professionals always have children
b) GPs can help parents socialise
c) Health visitors can help with childcare
d) Professionals have lots of experience

(1 mark)

Answers to the Reading Questions

Section One — Finding Information in Texts

Page 5

Q1 a — A swimming club
Q2 c — Tells you about cycling
Q3 b — Advertises a cleaning job
Q4 d — An internet café

Page 7

Q1 b — The last 5 years
Q2 c — The council
Q3 September
Q4 At rush hour
Q5 Visit the website

Page 9

Q1 You could write any of these:
- Heart attacks
- Choking
- Bleeding
- Broken bones
- Burns

Q2 On the day
Q3 Joe Thandie
Q4 How to book
Q5 b — Five
Q6 Telephone 0181 564 2398

Page 11

Q1 You could write any of these:
- Puffins
- Fulmars
- Arctic terns
- Sea eagles
- Gannets
- Pacific gulls

Q2 • Beautiful coastline
• Interesting wildlife
Q3 c — 1.30 pm
Q4 Life jackets
Q5 August

Section Two — Advice for the Reading Test

Page 13

Q1 d — 300
Q2 a — £50 of theatre vouchers
Q3 St Crispin's Hospice
Q4 Call Mark
Q5 11th November

Page 15

Q1 a) Any correct definition is acceptable. For example 'allowed by an authority'
b) Any correct definition is acceptable. For example 'stand for'
c) Any correct definition is acceptable. For example 'exact or careful'
Q2 Any correct definition is acceptable. For example 'forbid or not allow'
Q3 Any correct definition is acceptable. For example 'expert'
Q4 Any correct definition is acceptable. For example 'oversee or watch over'

Reading Test Practice

You should aim for around six or more marks out of eight in each reading exercise to pass.

Source A (Pages 18-19)

Q1 Spark Bridge Pool
Q2 • Dedicated
• Positive
• Friendly
Q3 c — Tuesday and Thursday
Q4 c — Swimming coaches
Q5 Joining the Club
Q6 Jim Davies

Source B (Pages 20-21)

Q1 b — The village school
Q2 14th July
Q3 £2
Q4 • Prizes
• Vouchers
Q5 A cake stall
Q6 • If they want to bake a cake
• If they want to donate a prize

Source C (Pages 22-23)

Q1 Any correct definition is acceptable. For example, 'alter or change'
Q2 1988
Q3 • Highly-skilled sewing
• Good value for money
Q4 £10
Q5 d — 3 pm
Q6 £20
Q7 a — Ironing

Source D (Pages 24-25)

Q1 It has a warm atmosphere
Q2 The local area
Q3 • Prawn cocktail
• Tomato and basil soup
Q4 Grilled salmon
Q5 You could write either of these:
• Rich chocolate fudge cake
• Summer fruits cheesecake
Q6 £13
Q7 b — Chocolate cake

Source E (Pages 26-27)

Q1 b — To tell you how to grow herbs

Q2 On a windowsill

Q3 • Thyme
- Basil
- Parsley

Q4 Enough to cover them

Q5 c — Fill the pot with compost

Q6 The back of the packet

Source F (Pages 28-29)

Q1 b — Save money on train tickets

Q2 You could write either of these:
- It is good for the environment
- It is less stressful than cars

Q3 a — Tickets are expensive

Q4 You could write any two of these:
- Book in advance
- Order online
- Compare prices
- Buy a railcard
- Buy a weekly ticket
- Buy a monthly ticket

Q5 You could write either of these:
- Because it will be cheaper
- Because the price goes up as the date of your journey gets closer

Q6 • Go to the ticket office
- Call the Travel Helpline

Source G (Pages 30-31)

Q1 b — Quotes include all costs

Q2 c — Moves for old people

Q3 Replace it as quickly as possible

Q4 • Telephone
- Email

Q5 Any correct definition is acceptable. For example 'in one piece'

Q6 You could write any two of these:
- Careful
- Friendly
- Supportive

Source H (Pages 32-33)

Q1 a — Fill in an application form.

Q2 d — Answer all the questions

Q3 Read the instructions

Q4 • Teamwork
- Managing your time

Q5 • A recent employer
- A teacher
- A tutor

Source I (Pages 34-35)

Q1 b — A country house

Q2 The rose garden

Q3 Facilities

Q4 Summer

Q5 You could write any three of these:
- Dressing up in historical costumes
- Prizes
- Treasure hunts
- Games
- Assault course

Q6 d — Go to the website

Source J (Pages 36-37)

Q1 a — Advises people on safe winter driving.

Q2 There is often ice and snow on the roads.

Q3 You could write any three of these:
- Blanket
- Small shovel
- Torch
- Warm clothes
- Waterproof boots

Q4 d — It will take you longer to stop

Q5 Avoid driving

Q6 The emergency services

Source K (Pages 38-39)

Q1 The town centre

Q2 b — Monday to Wednesday

Q3 You could write any two of these:
- Serving customers
- Answering the phone
- Checking stock
- Checking stock prices
- Keeping the shop clean and tidy
- Helping other staff

Q4 b — Have previous experience

Q5 You could write any two of these:
- Confident
- Hard working
- A good leader

Q6 Call Gita

Source L (Pages 40-41)

Q1 b — Children can usually go to parent groups

Q2 Any correct definition is acceptable. e.g. 'a chance'

Q3 • Look for parent groups
- Phone your local council
- Go to a park

Q4 By phoning your local council

Q5 Where can I get support?

Q6 d — Professionals have lots of experience

Who you are Writing To and Why

Read the question carefully

1) It will tell you **who** you are writing to.
2) It will also tell you **why** you are writing to them.
3) You can **use** this information when you write your **answer**.

You need to know who you are writing to

This will tell you what kind of **language** to use.

EXAMPLE 1:

1) Write a piece for your local newspaper about the opening of a new hospital.

You are writing to the people who read that newspaper.

EXAMPLE 2:

1) Write an email to your friend to invite them to the cinema with you next week.

You are writing to your friend.

You need to know why you are writing

This will tell you **what** to write **about**.

EXAMPLE 1:

1) Write an advert for an online auction site to sell your bike.

You are writing to give people information about your bike. You need to give details about it.

EXAMPLE 2:

1) Write your personal statement for this job.

You are writing to tell the company why they should give you the job. You need to write about your skills and work experience.

Practice Questions

1) For each of these writing tasks write down **who** you are writing to.

a) Write a letter to the council to tell them about problems in your area.

Who are you are writing to? ....

b) You are doing a charity bike ride. Write an email to your friends to tell them about it.

Who are you are writing to? ....

c) Write a letter to your electricity supplier to complain about their new prices.

Who are you are writing to? ....

d) You are organising the work Christmas party, and you need to invite the whole company. Write an email to tell everyone what you have arranged.

Who are you are writing to? ....

2) For each of these writing tasks write down **why** you are writing.

a) You want to paint your house. Write an email to your landlord to ask him if you can.

Why are you are writing? ....

b) You need sponsorship for your charity swim.
Write a note for the notice board at work, telling people how to sponsor you.

Why are you are writing? ....

c) Your flight home was delayed. Write a complaint on the airline's webpage.

Why are you are writing? ....

d) Write a letter to your local playgroup offering to volunteer once a week.

Why are you are writing? ....

Writing to Different People

Sometimes you write to people you know

1) Use more **chatty language** when you write to people you **know**.
2) For example, you might have to write to your **friends** or **family**.

EXAMPLE 1:

> Hi Kate,
> Are you busy on Friday? If you are free, I thought we could go and have a look at that flat. What do you think?

When writing to a friend, you use more chatty language.

EXAMPLE 2:

> I would definitely recommend that you go to Crete. It was awesome and the kids loved it.

You can use slang when you know the person you're writing to. For example, the slang 'kids' instead of 'children'.

3) You should **never** use **text language** like 'cos' or 'tho' in the test.

Sometimes you write to people you don't know

1) Use **serious** language when you write to people you **don't know**.
2) You should also use it for people you know who are **important**, like your manager at work.
3) Serious writing **sounds** more **professional**.

EXAMPLE 1:

> Dear Mrs Harris,
> I am writing to see if you are available on Friday. I would like to arrange a time to view the flat for rent.

When you write to somebody you don't know, you use more serious language.

EXAMPLE 2:

> I would suggest Crete for a family holiday. It is always popular with our customers and their children.

When writing to people you don't know, don't use slang. For example, write 'children' instead of 'kids'.

Practice Questions

For each writing task there are two options for how to start the answer.
Choose the one that **sounds best** for each task, and circle its letter.

1) Write a letter to thank a relative for a present they gave you.

    a) Hi Aunt Milly, I love the beautiful photo album you sent me. Thanks so much.

    b) Dear Mrs Samson, I am writing to thank you for the photo album I received.

2) Write a personal statement to apply for a job as a childcare assistant.

    a) I really want to have this job. I am brilliant with kids, so I would be a great choice.

    b) I am applying for the childcare assistant position. I have lots of childcare experience.

3) Write an email to your manager asking for two weeks off.

    a) Dear John, I would like to request two weeks of annual leave at the end of August.

    b) Hi John, I'm off on my hols in Spain soon. Can you sort out some leave for me?

4) You were too busy to contact your friend at the weekend. Write a letter to apologise.

    a) Dear Mr Kent, I would like to apologise for not contacting you this weekend.

    b) Hi Dave, I'm so sorry I didn't get in touch this weekend.

5) Write an email to invite people to your friend's birthday party.

    a) It's Sarah's 25th birthday next week. We are throwing her a surprise party.

    b) I would like to inform everyone that it will be Sarah's 25th birthday next week.

6) You see a job advertised. Write an email to the company asking for more information.

    a) Dear Sir or Madam, I have seen your job advert, and I am interested in the post.

    b) Hello, I've seen your poster. The job looks really good.

What to Include in your Writing

Use the bullet points for ideas about what to write

1) You will usually be given **bullet points** underneath the writing task.
2) Use them to tell you **what** to write about.

EXAMPLE:

1) You are organising a charity day. Write an article telling people what will be happening.

   You could include:

   - Where it will be
   - What events will be held
   - What it is raising money for

You need to write about these things.

You might have to make up some details

1) You can use details from the **question** in your writing.
2) You will probably need to **make up** some sensible details.

EXAMPLE:

1) You are unhappy with the service you have received from your mobile phone network. Write a letter asking to cancel your phone contract.

   You could include:

   - Why you are writing
   - Why you are unhappy
   - When you would like your contract to end

You know this from the question. You are writing to cancel your phone contract.

You need to make up details here. For example, as soon as possible or at the end of the month.

You need to make up details here. For example, you have poor signal or you can never get through to customer services.

Practice Questions

Each question below has a writing task and four ideas about what to include. Choose the writing that gives the **best answer** to the task, and circle its letter.

1) Write an advert to sell your bookshelf.

You should include:
- A description of the bookshelf
- How much you are selling it for

a) Bookshelf for sale. Two metres tall and made of oak. A great deal at £30.

b) Bookshelf for sale. A desk, an armchair and a coffee table also available.

c) Furniture for sale. £40. Contact linda@speedymail.co.uk for details.

d) Furniture for sale. Five feet tall. Made of black plastic.

2) Your train was 20 minutes late. Write a letter of complaint to the train company.

You should include:
- How the delay affected you
- What you want them to do about it

a) Your trains are very dirty. I think you should clean the carriages more often.

b) The standard of service on your trains is terrible. I now drive to work if possible.

c) Yesterday, a late train made me late for work. I would like a refund.

d) Your trains are always late. They often make me late for appointments.

3) Write a letter to the council to suggest an improvement to your area.

You should include:
- What improvement you think they should make
- Why they should make this improvement

a) There are lots of problems in this area. Please make some improvements.

b) The main road needs resurfacing. It is a busy road, and there are many potholes.

c) I am not happy with the potholes on the streets in the town centre.

d) The council should make some improvements to the bus shelter.

Putting Things in the Right Order

Think about what order you say things in

1) Write your points in a **sensible order**.
2) This will make it easier for the reader to **understand** what you're saying.

Group similar information together

1) Write **everything** about **one point** first, and then move on to the **next point**.
2) **Don't** go back to writing about the first point again.

EXAMPLE:

You are running a race to raise money for charity.
Write an email to your friend to tell them about it.

I am running a marathon to raise money for charity. I am hoping to raise about £600. I have asked everyone I know to sponsor me.

I have been training for five months. I go for a run before work every day, and I go to the gym twice a week.

Here, the text talks about raising money for charity.

Here, the text is about the training for the marathon. There is no information about raising money.

Write your most important point first

This tells the reader what you are writing about **straight away**.

EXAMPLE 1:

Car for sale. Blue Ford Mondeo. £2500.

The most important point is that a car is for sale.

EXAMPLE 2:

You are all invited to dinner at my house on Saturday. Come any time after 8 pm.

The most important point is the invitation to dinner.

Practice Questions

In each question there is a writing task and three points to include in the answer. Write out the points, putting them in the **best order**.

1) Write a personal statement to apply for a carpentry course.

- Say how the course would be helpful for your future
- Talk about the skills and experience you have
- Say that you want to apply for the course

a) ....

b) ....

c) ....

2) You are making cakes for a cake stall. Write an email to a friend asking them to help.

- Ask them to bake some cakes
- Tell them when the cakes should be ready by
- Tell them about the cake stall

a) ....

b) ....

c) ....

3) Write a letter to the town hall asking to use a room for your first aid course.

- Say how the course would be good for the community
- Say you would like to use the room for your course
- Give details of when you would like to use the room

a) ....

b) ....

c) ....

How to Write a Plan

Make a plan before you start writing

1) A plan will help you put your ideas **in order**.
2) Write down any points you can think of which **answer the question**.
3) You **don't** have to use full sentences in your plan.
4) You will often get **marks** for writing a plan.
5) **Check** your plan when you are writing your draft so you **don't miss anything**.

There are different ways of planning

Here is a task and **two** ways of **planning** your answer.

EXAMPLE:

1) Write an email to your landlord telling him about the problems in your flat.

1) You could draw a **spider diagram**.

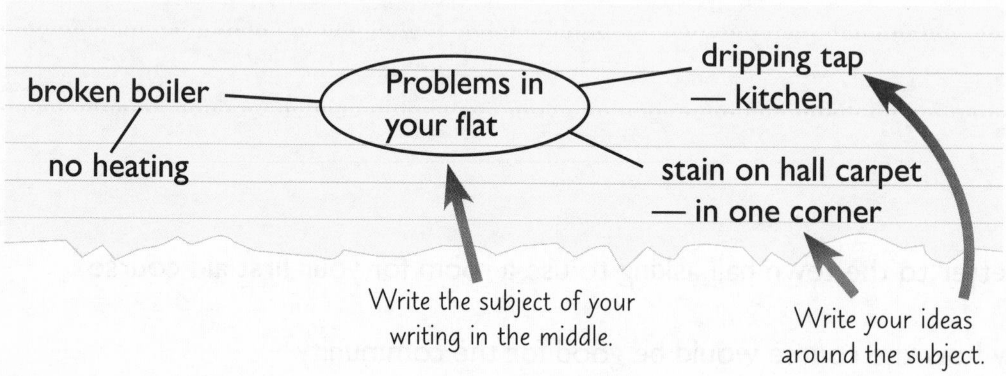

2) Or you could make a **list** of all the points you want to make.

Write your most important point first.

1. Boiler is broken — heating won't work
2. Kitchen tap drips
3. Stain on hall carpet

Practice Question

1) The company you work for offers an award for the 'Employee of the Year'. The award goes to someone who is hardworking and who does tasks that are not part of their job.

Your work friend is always helping others and goes out of their way to make sure every task is done properly. You decide to nominate them for the award.

Plan a piece of writing to say why your friend should be the 'Employee of the Year'.

You could include:

- Details about your friend. For example, how long they have worked for the company.
- Why you think your friend is a good employee.

Write your plan here:

Drafting and Checking

Use your plan to make a first draft

1) You might be asked to write a **draft answer**.
2) Put the ideas in your plan into **full sentences**.
3) Group sentences about the **same thing** into **paragraphs**.
4) Use the same **order** you decided on in your plan.

See p.56 for more about using paragraphs.

Read your first draft carefully

1) Take out anything you **don't need**.
2) Add in extra details that **improve** your answer.
3) Check that your **spelling**, **punctuation** and **grammar** are correct.

EXAMPLE:

1) Many street lights in your town are broken and have not been fixed.
   Write a letter to your local council asking them to improve street lighting.

Add details.

Make your writing sound better.

Dear Sir/Madam,

I am writing to ask you to ~~do something about~~ *improve* the street lighting in ~~town~~ *Southfield town centre*. Many street lights ~~are broke~~ *are broken* and have not been fixed. A lot of people do not feel safe walking at night.

Please fix the street lights ~~becos~~ *because* it might lower crime.

Check your grammar.

Check your spelling.

Check the final draft for mistakes

1) Once you have corrected your first draft, write out your final answer.
2) Read through it once more to check for mistakes.

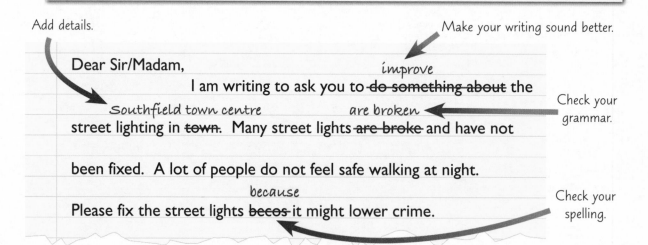

Practice Question

1) Here is a writing task and a plan.

You want to go to the cinema for your birthday.
Write an email inviting your friends to come with you.

<u>Who to</u>: friends   <u>Why</u>: invitation

<u>Details</u>

- What: Birthday trip — to watch 'Blue Boy'
- When: July 16th, 8pm
- Where: Cinema — directions

<u>Anything else</u>

- Reply by Friday — so I can book tickets.

Turn this plan into a first draft. Then make improvements and add details.

....

....

....

....

....

....

....

....

....

....

....

....

....

....

....

Using Paragraphs

A paragraph is a group of sentences

1) These sentences talk about the **same thing** or **follow on** from each other.
2) Start a new paragraph on a **new line**.

with no respect for anyone else living in the street.

I have tried to speak to them many times, but it has not worked. They don't listen to me, and get angry. ← This is the end of one paragraph.

We really cannot carry on like this. I do not want to be forced out of my own home. Please can you visit them, and make it clear that they need to

This is the start of a new paragraph. Leave a space at the beginning of the first line. Or you could leave a line blank.

Paragraphs make your writing clearer

1) Give each **point** in your plan its own **paragraph**.
2) Your first paragraph should say **what** your answer is **about**.
3) The middle paragraphs should add more **details**.
4) Your last paragraph should **sum up** your main point.

Start a new paragraph when something changes

Start a new paragraph when you talk about a different **thing**, **person**, **place** or **time**.

I am friendly and enjoy working with other people. This would be useful for working in your salon.

I studied hairdressing at college and have learnt how to style different types of hair.

I worked in a beauty salon after college. This has taught me

This sentence is about a different thing, so it is in a new paragraph.

This sentence is about a different time, so it is in a new paragraph.

Practice Question

1) Read this piece of writing about winter celebrations.
   Rewrite it underneath, dividing it into **three** paragraphs.

> People all over the world celebrate the start of the new year. They count the seconds until midnight on the 31st of December, to mark the start of a new calendar year. Hogmanay is a Scottish celebration which is also held on the 31st of December. Some people carry on the celebrations until the 2nd of January, which is also a bank holiday in Scotland. Chinese New Year falls on a different date each year, and is celebrated in at least nine countries. The festivities last for around two weeks.

Writing Letters

Letters have a greeting at the top and a sign-off at the bottom

1) For someone you **don't know**:
    - Use a greeting like **'Dear Mr Jones'** if you know their name.
    - If you don't know their name, write **'Dear Sir or Madam'**.
    - End with **'Yours sincerely'** if you know their name or **'Yours faithfully'** if you don't.
2) For somebody you **know well**:
    - Use a greeting like **'Dear Sarah'** or **'Hi Mark'**.
    - End with **'Best wishes'** or **'See you soon'**.

Follow the rules for writing letters

1) Use **serious language** in letters to someone **important** or someone you **don't know**.
2) You should be **polite** to create a good impression.
3) If you are writing to a **friend** or **family member**, you can use **chatty** language.
4) Write your letter in **paragraphs**.

EXAMPLE:

Write this if you don't know the person's name.

Use the person's name if you know it. For example, 'Dear Mr Kenning'.

The first paragraph should say why you are writing.

Dear Sir or Madam,

I am writing to tell you that I am moving house.

My new address is 62 Time Street, Hightown, GG1 5TT.

I will be moving on 17th March, so my old address will not be in use after this date.

Please send any information to my new address.

Yours faithfully,

Mrs Dawn Starling

The middle paragraphs give more details. Each point has a new paragraph.

This is the sign-off. You're writing for someone you don't know, so it's 'Yours faithfully'.

The final paragraph says what you want them to do.

Write your full name at the bottom.

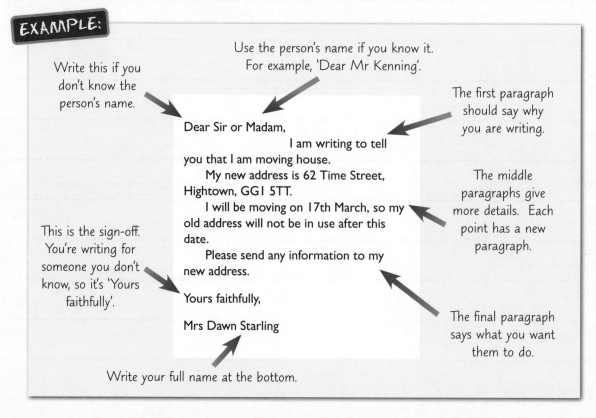

Practice Question

1) A bus company is planning to introduce a new bus service in your area.
You use the bus regularly, so extra services would be useful for you.

Write a letter to the company to tell them what you think about the new bus service.

You should include:

- Why you think the new bus service is a good idea
- When you think the new buses should run
- Who you think would use them

Dear ______________________________ ,

....

....

....

....

....

....

....

....

....

....

....

....

....

....

....

Writing Emails

Emails also start with a greeting and end with a sign-off

1) If you **know** the person, use a **greeting** like '**Dear Dad**' or '**Hi Hanif**'.
2) If you **don't** know them, write something like '**Dear Mr Ogden**' or '**Dear Sir or Madam**'.
3) If you **know** the person, use a **sign-off** like '**See you soon**'.
4) If you **don't** know them, write something like '**Many thanks**' or '**Yours sincerely**'.

Use paragraphs in your email

1) Your **first** paragraph should say **why** you are writing the email.
2) Write a **paragraph** in the email for **each** point in your plan.
3) Your **last** paragraph should say what you would like the person to **do**.

Lay out emails correctly

Fill in the boxes that you are given.

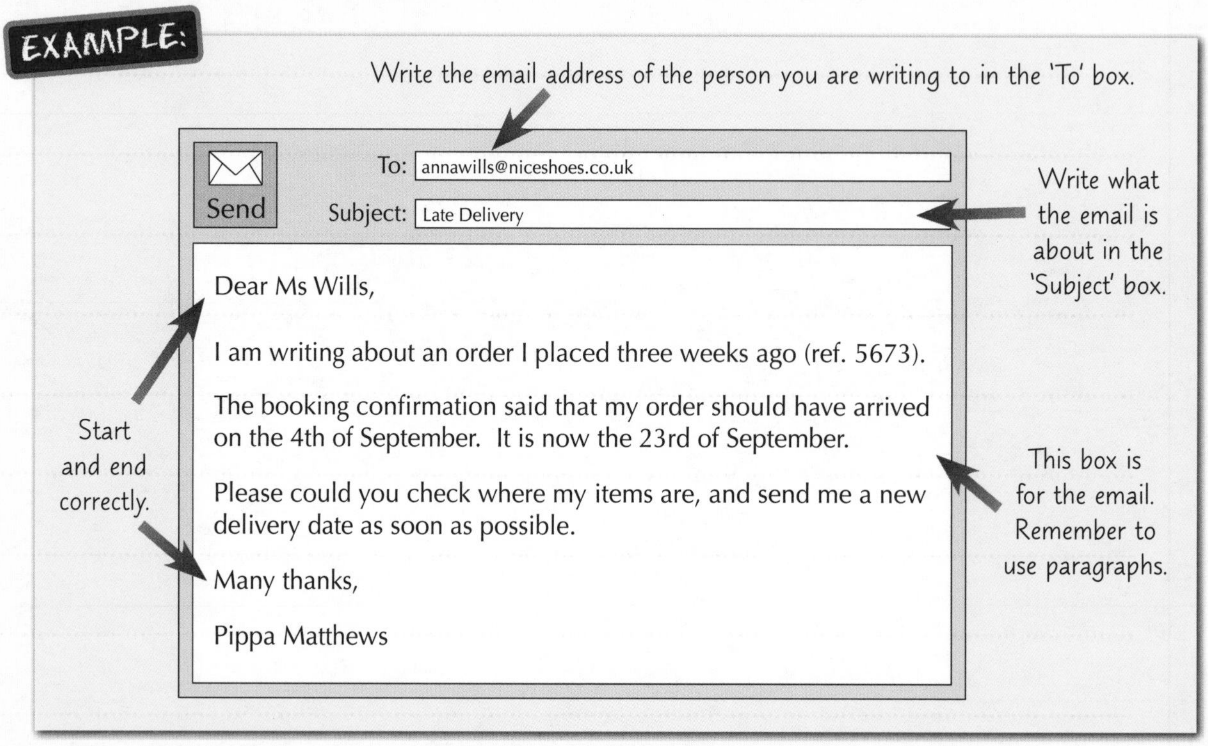
EXAMPLE:
Write the email address of the person you are writing to in the 'To' box.
Send
To: annawills@niceshoes.co.uk
Subject: Late Delivery
Write what the email is about in the 'Subject' box.
Dear Ms Wills,
I am writing about an order I placed three weeks ago (ref. 5673).
The booking confirmation said that my order should have arrived on the 4th of September. It is now the 23rd of September.
Please could you check where my items are, and send me a new delivery date as soon as possible.
Many thanks,
Pippa Matthews
Start and end correctly.
This box is for the email. Remember to use paragraphs.

Practice Question

1) Read this email from a work friend about changes to the canteen menu.

Send

From: steffburns@companyemail.co.uk

To: workers@companyemail.co.uk

Subject: New Menu

Hello everyone,

The canteen staff are making a new lunch menu. We have some ideas, but we want to make sure the options will suit as many people as possible.

Please could you send me suggestions of foods you would like to see on the menu. We would also like to know how often you buy food from the canteen.

Thanks,

Steff

Write a short reply which says:

- What you would like to see on the new menu
- How often you buy food from the canteen

Send

To:

Subject:

....

....

....

....

....

....

....

....

....

....

Filling in Forms

There are many types of form

1) You might have to fill in a form like a **job application form** or a **competition entry form**.
2) Fill in **every part** of the form. Write '**n/a**' if something doesn't apply to you.
3) If you are asked about your **education** or **jobs**, start with the **most recent** first.

Some answers will be very short

1) The first questions on forms usually need **short answers**.

EXAMPLE:

Name: ____________________ Date of Birth: ____________

Address: ____

____

2) You do not need to write in **full sentences** for **short** answers.

Some answers will be longer

1) For example, 'Why do you think you would be good at this job?'
2) You will have a much **bigger space** to write in.

EXAMPLE:

Explain what happened:

You will need to write a few paragraphs for longer answers.

3) You need to write in **full sentences**.
4) Make a **plan** before writing longer answers.

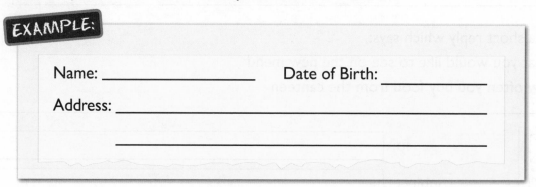

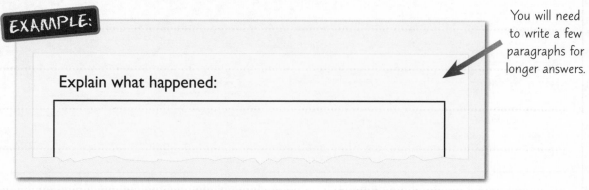

Practice Question

1) You want to apply to be a customer service assistant at a call centre. The company is looking for people who are fast learners and who have basic computer skills and good communication skills.

Fill in the application form below.
You can make up realistic details if you need to.

You could include:

- Why you would like the job
- Any work experience you have
- Any other useful skills you have

Happy Chatting Call Centres

Name: ______ Date of birth: ______

Position applied for: ______

Why are you right for this job?

....

....

....

....

....

....

....

....

....

....

....

Writing Instructions

Instructions are written in the order they will be done

1) Instructions are often written as **numbered points** or **bullet points**.

2) They should always be written in the **order** they need to be done.

See p.10 for more on bullet points.

EXAMPLE:

Sponge Cake Recipe

1. Weigh out the butter, sugar and flour.
2. Mix them together and add the eggs.
3. Pour the mixture into a greased cake tin.
4. Bake for 30 minutes at 180°C.

These instructions are written as numbered points.

These instructions would be impossible to follow if they were in the wrong order.

Instructions need to be clear

1) **Simple language** makes instructions **easy** to understand.

2) There is not much **description**. This makes the points **clearer**.

EXAMPLE 1:

Directions from the church to the wedding reception

- Turn left at the end of Church Street.
- Continue until the roundabout.
- Take the first exit onto George Street.
- When you get to the primary school, turn right.
- The Fairfield Hotel will be on your left.

Instructions are usually broken up into short sentences.

EXAMPLE 2:

If the fire alarm sounds:

- Leave the building quickly and calmly.
- Do not go back for your belongings.
- Meet at the carpark.

These instructions don't give any details that are not needed.

Practice Question

1) The paragraphs below tell you how to put up a shelf.

<u>Putting up a shelf</u>

Decide where you want your shelf to be, and mark the position of the brackets on the wall with a pencil. Use a spirit level to make sure that the brackets will be level. Then, drill some holes into the wall ready for the screws to fit into.

Using a screwdriver, screw the brackets to the wall, making sure that the screws are fairly tight. Attach the shelf to the brackets with more screws, making sure that they will not move when the shelf is being used.

Rewrite the paragraphs as instructions. Make each instruction as simple as possible. Use bullet points to make your instructions clearer.

....

....

....

....

....

....

....

....

....

....

....

....

....

....

....

Writing Reports

Reports are pieces of factual writing

1) This means that they contain lots of **information**.
2) For example, an **accident report**, a **personal statement** for a job or a **newspaper article**.
3) You are usually writing to someone you **don't know**, so your writing should not be chatty.

A personal statement is a piece of writing about yourself and your skills. They are usually written to apply for a job or a college course.

Organise your ideas by writing a plan

Think about **why** you are writing the report, and write notes about the **important facts**.

EXAMPLE:

1) You left your purse on the bus. Write down some information for the bus company telling them what happened and what your purse is like.

You need to tell the bus company about your lost purse.

- Bus 6B Monday 6th October, 10.30 am.
- Yellow purse.
- Cards inside.
- Contact me if you find it.

You should include facts like the date and time you lost your purse and what it looks like.

Write your report using your plan

1) Start a new **paragraph** for each new **point**.
2) You might want to **divide** your report into **sections.**

Separating the information into sections makes it easier to read.

<u>Incident</u>
I left my purse on bus 6B on Monday 6th October. The bus left the station at 10.30 am. I left it on a seat near the front of the bus.
<u>Description</u>
A yellow, woman's purse. There are cards and my driving licence inside. There is photo of my daughter in the side pocket.

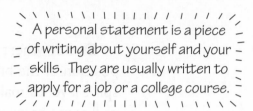

Practice Question

1) You organised a charity fundraising day at work. You receive this email from a work friend:

Send

From: mike@tatesimpson.co.uk

Subject: Fundraising day report

Hello,

Your fundraising day was brilliant. I hope you raised lots of money.

Could you write a short report about the day for the company newsletter?

You could include a bit about the day itself, how much money you raised and what the hospital will spend the money on.

Thank you,
Mike

Write a report about the fundraising day using the suggestions in the email.
Divide your writing into sections to make it clearer.

Making Sentences

Always write in sentences

1) You get marks for using **full sentences** in the writing test.
2) You **don't** need to use full sentences in your **plan**. Use notes instead.
3) If you have to write a **draft**, you should use **full sentences**.

A sentence must make sense on its own

1) Every sentence needs an **action word**. This is called a **verb.**

EXAMPLE:

Every morning my neighbour runs to work.

This is the verb. It tells you what happens.

2) A sentence needs **someone** or **something** to 'do' the verb.

EXAMPLE:

The machine is 'doing' the action.

The machine makes small parts for cars.

3) Some sentences tell you **who** or **what** the action is being **done to**.

EXAMPLE:

I sold my coin collection yesterday.

The selling was 'done' to the coin collection.

Make sentences by putting all the parts together

Put the person or thing **doing** the action and the **verb** together.

EXAMPLE:

This is the verb.

The shopping centre is 'doing' the action.

The shopping centre | closes | at 11 pm.

This adds detail.

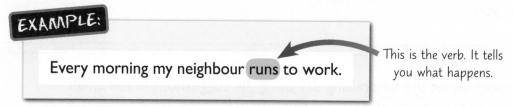

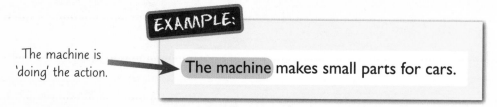

Practice Questions

1) Underline the verb in each sentence.

   a) Our manager writes the timetable.

   b) My neighbour organised a party.

   c) I applied for the job today.

   d) We eat our lunch in the canteen.

   e) At college I studied to be an electrician.

2) Underline who or what is doing the action in each sentence.

   a) The car broke down on the way to work.

   b) Our cat caught a mouse.

   c) You cycled to work last week.

   d) I read the application form.

   e) My sister works in a bank.

3) Read these notes giving details of a computer course. Rewrite the notes in full sentences.

   Starts 9 am, ends 5 pm
   Lunch break 1 pm
   Two coffee breaks
   Bring pen and notebook.

   ....

   ....

   ....

   ....

   ....

   ....

   ....

Punctuating Sentences

Sentences start with capital letters

Every sentence should begin with a **capital letter**.

EXAMPLE 1:

The price of petrol keeps rising.

EXAMPLE 2:

Men were working on the road. That is why I was late for work.

Names also start with capital letters

1) Names of **people** and **places** begin with capital letters.

EXAMPLE:

Fiona is going to America soon.

2) The **days** of the week and **months** of the year also start with capital letters.

EXAMPLE:

Next Tuesday is the last day in January.

3) **'I'** is **always** a capital letter when you are talking about yourself.
4) **Don't** use capital letters in the **middle** of a word.

Sentences end with full stops

Use a **full stop** to show that your sentence has **finished**.

EXAMPLE:

The car kept rattling. He pulled over.

You need a full stop and a capital letter every time you finish one sentence and start another.

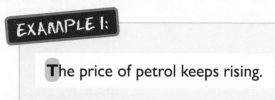

Punctuating Sentences

Questions end with question marks

1) A question should **start** with a **capital letter**.
2) It should end with a **question mark** instead of a full stop.

EXAMPLE:

Are you tired**?**

Use a question mark here.
You don't need a full stop as well.

Practice Question

1) Use capital letters, full stops and question marks to write these sentences correctly.

a) the dentist only had an appointment for friday

....

b) My manager said i could take the day off

....

c) who should i write a letter to

....

d) i am going on holiday to turkey

....

e) would you like to join our tennis club

....

f) we want to go to cornwall for our holiday.

....

g) does this train go directly from portsmouth to York

....

h) i am going to the cinema with anita tonight.

....

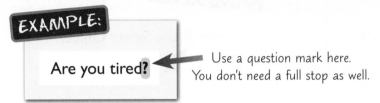

Writing About Different Times

A verb is a 'doing' or 'being' word

Use verbs to describe what something **does** or **is**.

EXAMPLE 1:

I buy petrol every week.

This is a 'doing' word.

EXAMPLE 2:

Jack is the Safety Officer.

This is a 'being' word.

Use the present tense to say what is happening now

Most verbs in the **present tense** follow the same **verb pattern**:

EXAMPLE:

If you are writing about 'I', 'you', 'we' or 'they', you don't need to change the verb.

I	make
you	make
we	make
they	make

he	makes
she	makes
it	makes

If you are writing about 'he', 'she' or 'it' you need to add an 's' to the end of the verb.

How you change the verb depends on who is doing it

Use the **verb pattern** to work out the correct ending.

EXAMPLE 1:

I make the bed.

The verb pattern shows that you don't need to change the verb when you are writing about 'I'.

EXAMPLE 2:

She makes cupcakes.

You need to add an 's' to the verb because you are talking about 'she'.

EXAMPLE 3:

They sell bicycles.

You don't need to change the verb when you are writing about 'they'.

EXAMPLE 4:

It sells furniture.

You need to add an 's' to the verb because you are talking about 'it'.

Writing About Different Times

Use the past tense to say what has already happened

1) For most verbs you need to add **'ed'** to the end to make them past tense.

EXAMPLE 1:

walk → I walked

EXAMPLE 2:

touch → You touched

2) If the verb already ends in **'e'**, just add a **'d'** to the end.

EXAMPLE 1:

hope → They hoped

EXAMPLE 2:

invite → We invited

Not all past tense verbs add 'ed'

You need to learn these verbs.

1) Some verbs follow their own **patterns**.

EXAMPLES:

Verb	Past Tense
I do	I did
I have	I had
I see	I saw
I get	I got
I take	I took

Verb	Past Tense
I am / we are	I was / we were
I go	I went
I make	I made
I come	I came
I think	I thought

Use 'was' for 'I', 'he', 'she' and 'it'. Use 'were' for 'you', 'we' and 'they'.

2) Some verbs **don't change** at all in the past tense.

EXAMPLES:

cut put hit set cost let

Writing About Different Times

To talk about the future you can use 'I am going'...

1) Talk about future actions by using the correct version of '**I am going**'.

I am going	
you are going	he is going
we are going	she is going
they are going	it is going

The 'going' part of the verb always stays the same.

EXAMPLE 1:

I am going to travel.

The 'I' is doing the travelling so you need to use 'am going'.

EXAMPLE 2:

We are going to eat.

The 'we' is doing the eating so you need to use 'are going'.

2) You need to put the word '**to**' **in front** of the action being done.

EXAMPLE 1:

He is going to drive.

EXAMPLE 2:

You are going to play golf.

...or you can use 'will'

1) You can also use '**will**' to talk about things in the future.

2) The 'will' part **never changes**. It doesn't matter **who** is doing the action.

EXAMPLE 1:

We will visit.

EXAMPLE 2:

He will visit.

The 'will' part is always the same and you don't have to change the verb that you put with it.

EXAMPLE 3:

They will go.

EXAMPLE 4:

She will go.

The only thing that changes is who does the action.

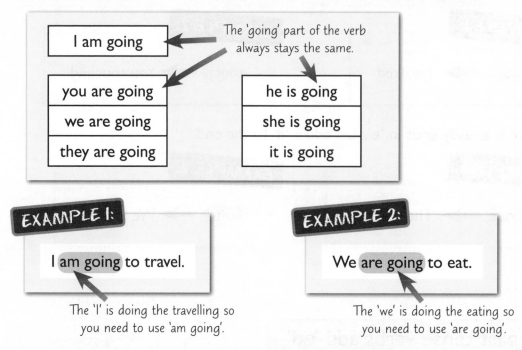

Practice Questions

1) These sentences are written in different tenses. Circle the correct tense for each one.

a) I went to the cinema. past present future

b) The sign says 'Stop'. past present future

c) You are going to go on holiday. past present future

d) They catch the bus to work. past present future

e) We will take photos to show you. past present future

2) Circle the correct verb to complete each sentence.

a) Belinda ***write / writes*** the article.

b) Simon ***cooks / cook*** pasta every day.

c) I ***washes / wash*** the car when it is sunny.

d) The trees ***was / were*** blowing in the wind.

e) You ***is / are*** organised today.

3) Rewrite these sentences so they make sense.

a) I buy four tomatoes but they were rotten.

....

b) We was at football yesterday.

....

c) I will catch the train, but I was still late.

....

d) You is going to go to the beach tomorrow.

....

e) They go to a meeting yesterday.

....

Common Mistakes with Verbs

The verb must match the person doing the action

Check **how many people** are doing the action to work out if the **verb** should **change**.

EXAMPLE 1:

Our printers often break. ← 'Printers' is plural (more than one), like 'we' or 'they'.

we	make
they	make

← Look at the verb table on p.70. If you are writing about 'we' or 'they' you don't change the verb.

Our printers often break. ← The verb stays as 'break'.

EXAMPLE 2:

Our printer often break. ← 'Printer' is singular (one), like 'he', 'she' or 'it'.

it	makes

← If you are writing about an 'it' you need to add an 's' to the verb.

Our printer often breaks. ← The verb becomes 'breaks'.

Use the right 'being' word to go with the person

1) Use '**is**' when you are talking about **one person** or **thing**.

2) Use '**are**' when you are talking about **more than one** person or thing.

EXAMPLE 1:

There is one security guard.

There is one security guard so use 'is'.

EXAMPLE 2:

There are two security guards.

There are two security guards so use 'are'.

'Been' and 'done' always go with 'have' or 'has'

Always use '**have**' or '**has**' when you write 'been' or 'done'.

EXAMPLE:

I have done the report you asked for.

You can't miss out the 'have' part. 'I done' doesn't make sense.

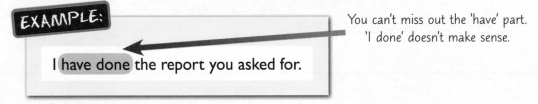

Common Mistakes with Verbs

Don't confuse 'could've' and 'could of'

1) Always write '**could have**'. Never write 'could of' because it doesn't mean anything.
2) It's the same for '**might have**' and '**should have**'.

EXAMPLE:

He could have cleaned the house. I should have told him to.

It's always 'could have'. You can't say 'could of' or 'could has'.

Practice Questions

1) The verb in each of these sentences is wrong. Rewrite the sentence with the correct verb.

a) The children plays in the park.

....

b) The fire alarm ring on Tuesdays.

....

c) She walk to the shops every day.

....

d) I throws away the bananas.

....

2) Rewrite each sentence so that it makes sense.

a) I could of done it yesterday, but I forgot.

....

b) You should of come to the party.

....

c) They done the shopping already.

....

Using Joining Words

Use joining words to make your writing sound better

Joining words **connect** two sentences together to make **one long sentence**.

EXAMPLE:

I like the outdoors. I enjoy hiking → I like the outdoors and I enjoy hiking.

'and' is used to join two separate sentences.

'Because' and 'so' add more detail

Use '**because**' and '**so**' to **explain** things.

EXAMPLE 1:

Mel is angry because her train is late.

The bit after 'because' explains why Mel is angry.

EXAMPLE 2:

Sam is on a diet so he can lose some weight.

The bit after 'so' explains why Sam is on a diet.

'But' and 'or' disagree with a point

1) Use '**but**' to **disagree** with something that's just been said.

EXAMPLE:

Marcus usually works the late shift, but he is in early today.

2) Use '**or**' to give **another option**.

EXAMPLE:

We could go clubbing tonight, or we could go bowling.

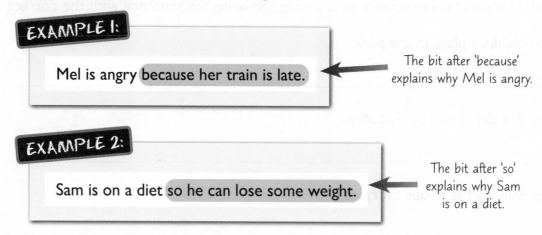

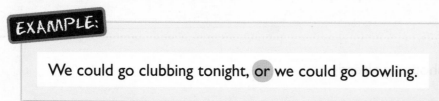

Practice Questions

1) Choose 'and', 'or', 'so', 'because' or 'but' to complete these sentences.

a) The college offers childcare courses .... it organises work placements.

b) She was late for work .... her alarm did not go off.

c) I want to buy a bike .... I can get fit.

d) They went to the shop .... it had already closed.

e) You should try this tea .... it is lovely.

f) I will either wear the blue shoes .... the pink shoes.

g) He built the cupboard carefully .... it was still a bit wobbly.

h) At the park, we saw Ryan .... he had his new dog with him.

2) Finish these sentences, adding an explanation.

a) I cannot come to work today because ....

b) I am going to buy a car so ....

c) She painted her room because ....

d) Do not go in the kitchen because ....

e) I woke up early so ....

f) I took the curtains back to the shop because ....

g) My brother is visiting me so ....

h) He brought his wallet so ....

Helpful Spelling Tips

The 'i' before 'e' rule

1) 'i' and 'e' often appear **next to each other** in a word.
2) This means it can be **tricky** to **remember** which comes **first**.
3) Use the **'i' before 'e' rule** to help:

'i' before 'e' except after 'c', but only when it rhymes with 'bee'.

EXAMPLE 1: believe
The 'ie' sound rhymes with bee, so 'i' goes before 'e'.

EXAMPLE 2: receive
The 'ie' sound rhymes with bee, but there's a 'c' so the 'e' goes before 'i'.

EXAMPLE 3: eight
The 'ie' sound doesn't rhyme with bee, so 'e' goes before 'i'.

EXAMPLE 4: science
The 'ie' sound comes after 'c', but it doesn't rhyme with bee, so 'i' goes before 'e'.

A few words don't follow the rule

If you're not sure about the spelling of a word, check your dictionary.

Watch out for these **tricky examples**.

EXAMPLE 1: weird seize caffeine
In these words, the 'ei' sound does rhyme with bee, but the 'e' still goes before the 'i'.

EXAMPLE 2: species
The 'i' goes before the 'e', even though it comes after 'c' and rhymes with bee.

Make up phrases to help you spell tricky words

Make up **sentences** or **phrases** to remind you how words are spelt.

EXAMPLE 1: Rhythm Has Your Two Hips Moving → rhythm
The first letter of each word in this phrase helps you spell 'rhythm'.

EXAMPLE 2: There's **a rat** in separate
Remembering smaller words can help you spell longer words.

Practice Questions

1) Rewrite each word so it is spelt correctly.

a) breif ....

b) wieght ....

c) peice ....

d) nieghbour ....

e) recieve ....

f) feild ....

2) These four words can be tricky to spell. Write down a phrase underneath each word to help you remember how to spell it.

because

....

....

could

....

....

weird

....

....

height

....

....

Making Plurals

Plural means 'more than one'

1) To make most words **plural** you put an **'s'** on the **end**.

EXAMPLE:

One car. Two cars.

The 's' means that there is more than one car.

2) If a word **ends** with **'ch'**, **'x'**, **'s'**, **'sh'** or **'z'**, put **'es'** on the **end** to make it plural.

EXAMPLES:

Two churches. Some boxes. Many dresses. Three wishes. The waltzes.

Words ending with 'y' have different rules

1) Some words end with a **vowel** ('a', 'e', 'i', 'o' or 'u') and then a **'y'**.

2) To make these words **plural**, put an **'s'** on the end.

EXAMPLES:

Two days. His keys. Five guys.

All these words end in a vowel and a 'y', so they just need an 's'.

3) Some words end with a **consonant** (any letter that isn't a **vowel**) and then a **'y'**.

4) To make them **plural**, change the **'y'** to **'ies'**.

EXAMPLE 1:

fly → flies

EXAMPLE 2:

city → cities

Words ending with 'f' or 'fe' need a 'v'

1) To make words ending with **'f'** or **'fe'** **plural** you need a **'v'**.

2) Take off the **'f'** or **'fe'** from the end of the word and add **'ves'** instead.

EXAMPLE 1:

one shelf → two shelves

EXAMPLE 2:

one wife → two wives

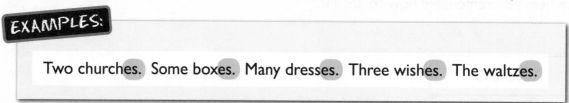

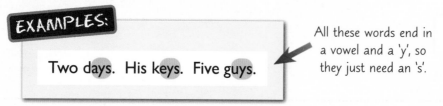

Making Plurals

Some words don't follow a pattern

1) To make some words plural you have to change the **spelling** of the word.

EXAMPLE 1: tooth → teeth

EXAMPLE 2: woman → women

EXAMPLE 3: mouse → mice

2) Some words **don't change at all**.

EXAMPLES:

fish deer sheep

You would always say 'two sheep', never 'two sheeps'.

Practice Questions

1) Write the plural of each word.

a) book ....

b) boy ....

c) sandwich ....

d) half ....

e) country ....

f) foot ....

2) Each sentence has an incorrect plural. Rewrite the sentence with the correct plural.

a) The loafs of bread I bought were too hard.

....

b) Can childs eat at your restaurant?

....

c) We are making two new dishs today.

....

d) I talked about my hobbys in the interview.

....

Adding Prefixes and Suffixes

Prefixes and suffixes are used to make new words

1) **Prefixes** are **letters** that are added to the **start** of words.

EXAMPLE 1:

un + lock → unlock

EXAMPLE 2:

re + appear → reappear

2) **Suffixes** are letters that are added to the **end** of words.

EXAMPLE 1:

love + ly → lovely

EXAMPLE 2:

hope + ful → hopeful

Prefixes and suffixes change the meaning of a word

When you add a **prefix** or a **suffix** it changes the **meaning** of the word.

EXAMPLE 1:

un + lucky → unlucky

EXAMPLE 2:

teach + er → teacher

Prefixes and suffixes can be tricky

1) There are a few prefixes that make a word mean the **opposite**.
2) For example, **un**, **in**, **im**, and **dis**. It's easy to get confused between them.

EXAMPLES:

impolite disorganised unhappy incorrect

Learn how to spell these words with prefixes.

3) Some **suffixes** can be hard to spell too.
4) **'ful'** is a common suffix. Words ending in 'ful' are always spelt with **one 'l'** at the end.

EXAMPLES:

successful helpful beautiful useful

Adding Prefixes and Suffixes

Adding a suffix might change the spelling

1) Adding a **prefix doesn't** change the spelling of a word.

EXAMPLE:

mis + spell → misspell

The spelling of the prefix and the word don't change.

2) If you add a **suffix** to a word, sometimes the spelling **changes**.

3) If a word ends in an **'e'** and the **first letter** of the suffix is a **vowel**, you **drop** the **'e'**.

EXAMPLE 1:

love + ing → loving

EXAMPLE 2:

care + er → carer

The vowels are 'a', 'e', 'i', 'o' and 'u'.

4) If a word ends with a **consonant** and then a **'y'**, change the **'y'** to an **'i'**.

EXAMPLE 1:

happy + ness → happiness

EXAMPLE 2:

dry + ed → dried

Practice Questions

1) Rewrite each word so it is spelt correctly.

a) dissagree ....

b) carefull ....

c) carryed ....

d) haveing ....

2) Each of these sentences has a mistake. Rewrite the sentence with the mistake fixed.

a) I remembered the file as I was leaveing.

....

b) The instructions were unecessary.

....

c) She tryed to phone the call centre again.

....

Common Spelling Mistakes

Words with double letters can be hard to spell

1) It's tricky to spell words with **double letters** because you **can't hear them.**
2) **Learn** how to spell these **common** words with **double letters**.

EXAMPLES:

address	necessary	tomorrow	success	eventually
different	possible	professional	immediately	occasionally

Silent letters and unclear sounds can be tricky

1) Sometimes you **can't hear** a certain **letter** when you say a word.
2) These are known as **silent letters**.

EXAMPLES:

when which write whole know could before surprise

3) Sometimes the **sound** in a word **isn't clear**.

Learn all these tricky spellings.

EXAMPLES:

because	company	decide	describe	horrible
business	complaint	definitely	experience	interesting

Make sure you are using the right word

1) '**A lot**' means '**many**'. '**Alot**' is **not** a word.
2) '**Thank you**' is always written as **two words**.
3) '**Maybe**' means '**perhaps**'. '**May be**' means '**might be**'.

If you can swap in 'might be', then you're using the right version of 'may be'.

EXAMPLE 1:

Maybe I'll come to the cinema.

EXAMPLE 2:

He may be coming to the cinema.

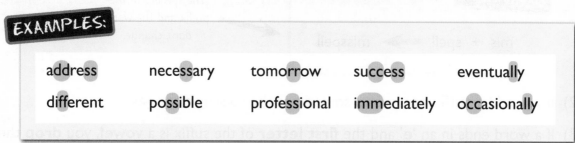

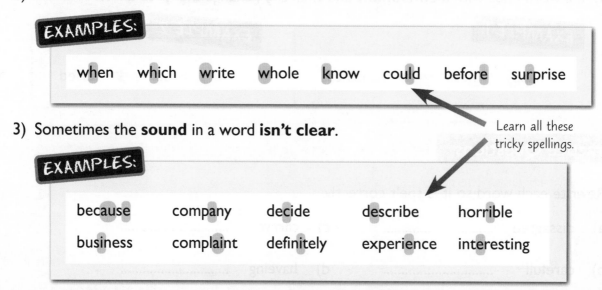

Practice Questions

1) Each of these sentences has a mistake. Rewrite the sentence with the mistake corrected.

a) Your order maybe ready to send tomorrow.

....

b) You must have previous experiance to apply.

....

c) We chose a diffrent route to work today.

....

d) Were are you going for dinner?

....

e) Thankyou so much for coming.

....

f) I suceeded in persuading him.

....

g) Shuld I drive the van?

....

h) We rote out the report.

....

2) Circle the correct word to use in each sentence.

a) ***Wat / What*** are you going to do when you arrive?

b) The garage has been doing really good ***busness / business*** this year.

c) Can you ***describe / discribe*** what the man looked like?

d) The ***hole / whole*** room was filled with people.

e) There are five boxes ***which / witch*** are kept in the freezer.

f) Everyone was happy ***when / wen*** they had an extra holiday.

g) I would like to make a ***complaint / complant*** about your staff.

Commonly Confused Words

'Their', 'they're' and 'there' are all different

1) **'Their'** means 'belonging to them'.

EXAMPLE 1:

Their flat has two bedrooms.

EXAMPLE 2:

He took their warning seriously.

2) **'They're'** means 'they are'.

EXAMPLE 1:

They're living in a two-bed flat.

EXAMPLE 2:

They're giving him a warning.

If you can replace 'they're' with 'they are' and the sentence still makes sense, then it is right.

3) **'There'** is used to talk about a **place**.

EXAMPLE 1:

The flat is over there.

EXAMPLE 2:

They are there now.

4) **'There'** can also **introduce a sentence**.

EXAMPLE 1:

There is no reason to give him a warning.

EXAMPLE 2:

There are two choices.

Learn how to use 'to' and 'too'

1) **'To'** can mean 'towards', or it can be part of a **verb**.

EXAMPLE 1:

He's going to Spain.

When 'to' means 'towards', it's followed by a place.

EXAMPLE 2:

He's going to come at 6 pm.

'To' is often followed by a verb.

2) **'Too'** can mean 'too much', or it can mean 'also'.

EXAMPLE 1:

This car is too slow.

This version of 'too' often has a describing word after it.

EXAMPLE 2:

He enjoyed the play too.

When 'too' means 'also', it usually comes at the end of a sentence.

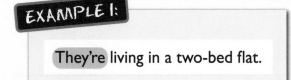

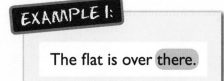

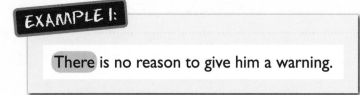

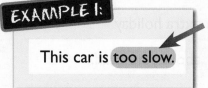

Commonly Confused Words

'Your' and 'you're' mean different things

1) '**Your**' means 'belonging to you'.

EXAMPLE:

Keep your uniform in your locker. ← The uniform belongs to you.

2) '**You're**' means 'you are'.

EXAMPLE:

You're working twice this week. ← If you can replace 'you're' with 'you are' and the sentence makes sense, then it's the right one.

Don't confuse 'know' and 'no'

1) '**Know**' means 'to be certain about something' or 'to be familiar with'.

EXAMPLE 1:

I know where it is.

EXAMPLE 2:

She knows my manager, Mr Onwe.

2) '**No**' means the opposite of yes.

EXAMPLE:

No, I can't give you a lift home.

'Are' and 'our' sound alike

See p.72 for more about verbs.

1) '**Are**' is a **verb**.

EXAMPLE 1:

We are paid every Friday.

EXAMPLE 2:

Are we going out tonight?

2) '**Our**' means 'belonging to us'.

EXAMPLE 1:

Our house is near the church.

EXAMPLE 2:

It's our favourite song.

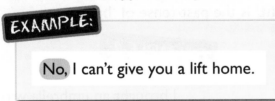

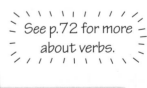

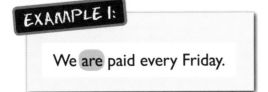

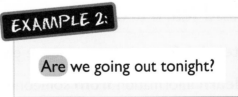

Commonly Confused Words

'Been' and 'being' can sound the same

1) '**Been**' always comes after the words '**have**', '**has**' or '**had**'.

EXAMPLE:

I have been there before. She has been too. Tom had been before us both.

2) '**Being**' always comes after '**am**', '**are**', '**were**' or '**was**'.

EXAMPLE 1:

I am being careful.

EXAMPLE 2:

They are being welcomed.

EXAMPLE 3:

We were being friendly.

EXAMPLE 4:

Josh was being protective.

'Bought' and 'brought' mean different things

See p.73 for more on the past tense.

'**Bought**' is the past tense of '**buy**'. '**Brought**' is the past tense of '**bring**'.

EXAMPLE 1:

I bought an umbrella at the shop.

EXAMPLE 2:

I brought an umbrella with me.

Teach and learn are opposites

1) You **teach** information **to** someone else.
2) You **learn** information **from** someone else.

EXAMPLE 1:

I teach French to my sister.

EXAMPLE 2:

My sister learns French from me.

Practice Questions

1) Circle the correct word to use in each sentence.

a) We've booked our family holiday ***to / too*** the Alps.

b) I have ***being / been*** thinking about buying a new car for a while.

c) Tim is ***learning / teaching*** the new trainees to use the software.

d) ***Our / Are*** workshop is really messy at the moment.

e) My girlfriend's parents work at the hospital. ***They're / Their*** both nurses.

f) Did you know you have left ***you're / your*** lights on?

g) Sina ***bought / brought*** the dog around to his Dad's house.

h) I left the vacuum cleaner over ***there / their*** by the cupboard.

2) Each of these sentences has a mistake. Rewrite the sentence with the mistake fixed.

a) The driver did not see the bike their.

....

b) You're handbag is in the locker.

....

c) I did not no that the bank was open today.

....

d) Are flat is above the pub.

....

e) I have always wanted to work for you're company.

....

f) Miriam bought cakes to the office.

....

g) I drove to close to the kerb.

....

Advice for the Writing Test

Read the question carefully before you start

1) There will be information in the **question** to help you think of what to write.

EXAMPLE:

> 1) You are organising a play with your drama club.
> Write an email to invite your friends to see it.

You have to write an email inviting your friends to see the play you are organising.

2) Make sure **everything** you write is to do with the question.

Plan and draft your work

1) You might get marks for **planning** and **drafting** your answer.
2) Planning helps you to **organise** your ideas.
3) **Don't** spend **too long** on your plan or your draft.
4) Leave enough time to write your **final copy**.

Don't spend all of your time on the first task

1) Make sure you leave enough **time** for **all** of the tasks you have to do.
2) You might have to do **two** tasks which are worth the **same** number of **marks**.
3) Spend **half** of the time on the **first** task and **half** of the time on the **second task**.
4) If one task has **more marks**, spend a bit **more time** on that one.

Use the right language

1) Always keep your writing **polite**.
2) Even if you are writing to complain about something, **don't be rude**.
3) **Don't** use **text language** like 'cos' or 'tho', even if you are writing to a friend.

Advice for the Writing Test

Write in full sentences

1) You get marks for writing in **full sentences**.
2) You should also use **paragraphs** to make your writing clearer.

Take care with spelling

1) You will be marked on your **spelling** in the writing test.
2) When you write a word that is in the **question**, make sure you spell it correctly.
3) If you don't know how to spell a word, **reword** your sentence so you don't use it.

EXAMPLE:

way I was treated

I would like to complain about the ~~service I received~~ when I bought a bag from your shop last week.

If you don't know how to spell 'received', you can change the sentence so you don't have to write it.

4) You can also use your **dictionary** to **check** your spelling if you have time.

Checking your work is important

1) If you have time at the end of the test, **check** your work for mistakes.
2) Make sure your answers **make sense**.
3) Check your **spelling**, **punctuation** and **grammar**.

There are lots of ways to answer a writing question

1) There isn't just **one right answer** to a writing question.
2) Just use the **bullet points** under the question to tell you what to write.
3) Everything you write should **link** to the **question**. Don't write things that are **not relevant**.

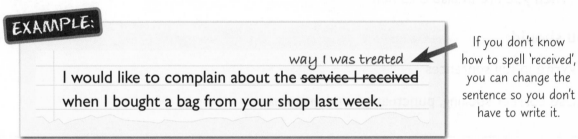

Exercise A — Volunteer Email

You have twenty minutes to complete this exercise. You may use a dictionary.
Your final answer should be about 100 words long. *(12 marks)*

You see a poster in the local animal shelter asking for volunteers and you would like to help.

Write an email to the manager asking to join her team.

You could write about:

- Why you are emailing her
- Why you would like to join the team
- Any relevant skills you have
- When you are available to help

You should:

- Write in full sentences
- Use correct spelling, punctuation and grammar

Plan your answer here:

Write your draft and your final answer on separate pieces of paper.

Exercise B — Competition Entry

You have twenty minutes to complete this exercise. You may use a dictionary.
Your final answer should be about 100 words long. *(12 marks)*

Your local estate agent is holding a competition. To win £200, you have to write about your dream house.

Write a piece to enter the competition.

You could write about:

- Where your house would be
- What rooms it would have
- What the garden would be like
- Any other features it would have

You should:

- Write in full sentences
- Use correct spelling, punctuation and grammar

Plan your answer here:

Write your draft and your final answer on separate pieces of paper.

Exercise C — Letter of Complaint

You have twenty minutes to complete this exercise. You may use a dictionary.
Your final answer should be about 100 words long. *(12 marks)*

You bought some cakes from the supermarket for a birthday party. However, when you got home you realised that the cakes were mouldy.

Write a letter to the supermarket to complain about what has happened.

You could write about:

- What the problem is
- When you bought the cakes
- Where you bought them from
- What you would like them to do about it

You should:

- Write in full sentences
- Use correct spelling, punctuation and grammar

Plan your answer here:

Write your draft and your final answer on separate pieces of paper.

Exercise D — Local Information

You have twenty minutes to complete this exercise. You may use a dictionary.
Your final answer should be about 100 words long. *(12 marks)*

Your friend is moving to the area, but does not know it very well.

Write an email giving them some information to help them settle in.

You could write about:

- Why you are emailing them
- What they could do at the weekend
- Where they can park in the town centre
- Where to find useful places like the post office or the supermarket.

You should:

- Write in full sentences
- Use correct spelling, punctuation and grammar

Plan your answer here:

Write your draft and your final answer on separate pieces of paper.

Exercise E — Personal Statement

You have twenty minutes to complete this exercise. You may use a dictionary.
Your final answer should be about 100 words long. *(12 marks)*

You see this advert in a shop window and you decide to apply.

Bakery assistant needed BARN BAKERY

Must be hardworking and friendly.

Hours: Monday to Saturday, 8 am to 5 pm.

Duties include helping with baking and serving customers.

Please hand a personal statement to Paul Price, the store manager.

Write a personal statement to give to the store manager.

You could write about:

- Why you would like to work at the bakery
- What experience you have
- Any other information about yourself

You should:

- Write in full sentences
- Use correct spelling, punctuation and grammar

Plan your answer here:

Write your draft and your final answer on separate pieces of paper.

Exercise F — Furniture Form

You have twenty minutes to complete this exercise. You may use a dictionary.
Your final answer should be about 100 words long. *(12 marks)*

You would like to sell your old sofa and you find this poster about a furniture shop.

Furniture Wanted

Dusty's Furniture Shop wants to buy your unwanted furniture. All pieces must be in good condition, but we are interested in almost everything. We will also collect items if you are nearby.

If you are interested, please fill in a form to tell us about the furniture, how much you want to sell it for, and where you live.

Write some information about your sofa to give to the shop.

You could write about:

- What the sofa is like
- How much you would like to sell it for
- Where you would like the sofa to be collected from

You should:

- Write in full sentences
- Use correct spelling, punctuation and grammar

Plan your answer here:

Write your draft and your final answer on separate pieces of paper.

Exercise G — Summer Holiday

You have twenty minutes to complete this exercise. You may use a dictionary.
Your final answer should be about 100 words long. *(12 marks)*

You want to go on a summer holiday with some friends.

Write an email to your friends asking them to come with you.

You could write about:

- When you would like to go
- Where you would like to go
- What you would like to do there
- When you would like them to reply by so you can book the tickets

You should:

- Write in full sentences
- Use correct spelling, punctuation and grammar

Plan your answer here:

Write your draft and your final answer on separate pieces of paper.

Exercise H — Feedback Form

You have twenty minutes to complete this exercise. You may use a dictionary.
Your final answer should be about 100 words long. *(12 marks)*

You stayed in a hotel for a weekend break and you were given a feedback form as you left.

Write some feedback for the hotel owners to tell them what you thought.

You could write about:

- What you thought about the rooms
- What you thought about the food
- How the staff treated you
- Whether you would stay there again

You should:

- Write in full sentences
- Use correct spelling, punctuation and grammar

Plan your answer here:

Write your draft and your final answer on separate pieces of paper.

Exercise 1 — Town Suggestions

You have twenty minutes to complete this exercise. You may use a dictionary.
Your final answer should be about 100 words long. *(12 marks)*

You see this notice in the Town Hall.

> As some of you will know, the computer shop on Walton Road has recently closed. The building is now empty, and we want to know what residents would like us to do with it.
>
> So far, suggestions have included a youth club, a bowling alley and an internet café. We want to know what you think of these ideas and whether you have any of your own. Please get in touch to let us know.
>
> TOWN HALL

Write down some suggestions for the new building.

You could write about:

- What you think of one of the suggestions so far
- What you think the building should be used for
- Why this would be good for the community

You should:

- Write in full sentences
- Use correct spelling, punctuation and grammar

Plan your answer here:

Write your draft and your final answer on separate pieces of paper.

Exercise J — Accident Report

You have twenty minutes to complete this exercise. You may use a dictionary.
Your final answer should be about 100 words long. *(12 marks)*

You twist your ankle at work and you see this poster on the notice board.

Accidents at Work

An accident report must be written whenever there is an accident at work. The report should include details of the accident and any injuries caused. All reports should then be handed to your line manager so they can decide whether any action is needed.

Write an accident report to give to your line manager.

You could write about:

- When and where the accident happened
- What happened and how badly you were hurt
- Whether you will need time off work

You should:

- Write in full sentences
- Use correct spelling, punctuation and grammar

Plan your answer here:

Write your draft and your final answer on separate pieces of paper.

Exercise K — Family Letter

You have twenty minutes to complete this exercise. You may use a dictionary.
Your final answer should be about 100 words long. *(12 marks)*

You are organising a family party to celebrate your parents' 30th wedding anniversary.

Write a letter to a family member inviting them to come.

You could write about:

- The date and time of the party
- Where the party will be
- What the party will be like
- Whether you need them to do anything

You should:

- Write in full sentences
- Use correct spelling, punctuation and grammar

Plan your answer here:

Write your draft and your final answer on separate pieces of paper.

Exercise L — Newspaper Article

You have twenty minutes to complete this exercise. You may use a dictionary.
Your final answer should be about 100 words long. *(12 marks)*

You are holding a music festival and you want to tell people about your plans.

Write a short piece for your local newspaper to tell people about the festival.

You could write about:

- Where and when the music festival will take place
- The type of music that will be playing
- What other attractions there will be
- How people can buy tickets

You should:

- Write in full sentences
- Use correct spelling, punctuation and grammar

Plan your answer here:

Write your draft and your final answer on separate pieces of paper.

Answers to the Writing Questions

Section One — What to Write About

Page 45

Q1 a) The council
b) Your friends
c) Your electricity supplier
d) The whole company

Q2 a) To ask if you can paint your house
b) To tell people how to sponsor you
c) To complain about your delayed flight
d) To offer to volunteer

Page 47

Q1 a — Hi Aunt Milly, I love the beautiful photo album you sent me. Thanks so much.

Q2 b — I am applying for the childcare assistant position. I have lots of childcare experience.

Q3 a — Dear John, I would like to request two weeks of annual leave at the end of August.

Q4 b — Hi Dave, I'm so sorry I didn't get in touch this weekend.

Q5 a — It's Sarah's 25th birthday next week. We are throwing her a surprise party.

Q6 a — Dear Sir or Madam, I have seen your job advert and I am interested in the post.

Page 49

Q1 a — Bookshelf for sale. Two metres tall and made of oak. A great deal at £30.

Q2 c — Yesterday, a late train made me late for work. I would like a refund.

Q3 b — The main road needs resurfacing. It is a busy road, and there are many potholes.

Page 51

Q1 a) Say that you want to apply for the course.
b) Talk about the skills and experience you have.
c) Say how the course would be helpful for your future.

Q2 a) Tell them about the cake stall.
b) Ask them to bake some cakes.
c) Tell them when the cakes should be ready by.

Q3 a) Say you would like to use the room for your course.
b) Give details of when you would like to use the room.
c) Say how the course would be good for the community.

Section Two — Planning and Drafting your Writing

Page 53

Q1 Your plan does not need to be in full sentences. You could include this information:
• Details about your friend. For example, Josh Vincent, trainee mechanic, worked at the company for 6 months.
• The things that make your friend a good employee. For example, hardworking — always makes sure tasks are done properly. Helpful — often helps other people at work.

Page 55

Q1 You should use full sentences to rewrite the plan. Here is an example of what you could write:

Hi everyone,

I'm going to go to the cinema for my birthday, and you are all invited. I thought we could see 'Blue Boy' on 16th July at 8 pm.
The cinema is on the Oakfield Retail Park, next to Big Burgers.

Please let me know by Friday if you can make it so I can book the tickets.

See you soon,
Mel

Page 57

Q1 You need to show that you have started a new paragraph by leaving a space at the beginning of the first line, or by leaving a line. Here is what you should have written:

People all over the world celebrate the start of the new year. They count the seconds until midnight on the 31st of December, to mark the start of a new calendar year.

Hogmanay is a Scottish celebration also held on the 31st of December. Some people carry on the celebrations until the 2nd of January, which is also a bank holiday in Scotland.

Chinese New Year falls on a different date each year, and is celebrated in at least nine countries. The festivities last for around two weeks.

Section Three — Different Types of Writing

Page 59

Q1 • You should write your answer in full sentences.
• You should start your letter with 'Dear Sir or Madam' because you do not know who you are writing to.
• You should end your letter with 'Yours faithfully' and your name.
You should include:
• Why you think the new bus service is a good idea. For example, many people rely on the bus to travel around town, it will mean that passengers have more travel options, or the new service would encourage more people to use the bus.
• When you think the new buses should run. For example, on the weekends or late at night.

• Who you think would use them. For example, shift workers, young people or people who cannot drive.

Page 61

Q1 • You should write Steff's email address in the 'To' box: steffburns@companyemail.co.uk.
• You should write what the email is about in the 'Subject' box.
• You should write your email in full sentences.
• Start your email with a greeting like 'Hello Steff'.
• You should end your email with a sign-off like 'Best wishes'.
You should include:
• What you would like to see on the new menu. For example, more vegetarian food.
• How often you buy food from the canteen. For example, every Friday.

Page 63

Q1 • The first three boxes on the application form only need short answers. For example, 'Ruth Riley', '02/05/87' and 'Customer Service Assistant'.
• For the longer answer you should write in full sentences. Under 'Why are you right for this job?' you could include:
• Why you would like the job. For example, you would like to improve your customer service skills.
• Any work experience you have. For example, working in a shop.
• What other useful skills you have. For example, you are good at dealing with problems or you are good at talking to people.

Page 65

Q1 Here is an example of what you could write:
• Mark the wall to show where you want to put the brackets.
• Use a spirit level to make sure that the brackets will be level.
• Drill holes into the wall for the screws.
• Screw the brackets to the walls.
• Screw the shelves to the brackets.

Page 67

Q1 Your report should be written in full sentences.
You should divide your writing into sections. For example:
• '<u>This Year's Charity Day</u>', including what happened on the day.
• '<u>Money Raised</u>', including how much money was raised this year, and whether it was any more than last year.
• '<u>What the money is for</u>', including what the hospital will spend the money on.

Section Four — Writing Sentences

Page 69

Q1 a) Our manager <u>writes</u> the timetable.
b) My neighbour <u>organised</u> a party.
c) I <u>applied</u> for the job today.
d) We <u>eat</u> our lunch in the canteen.
e) At college I <u>studied</u> to be an electrician.

Q2 a) The <u>car</u> broke down on the way to work.
b) Our <u>cat</u> caught a mouse.
c) <u>You</u> cycled to work last week.
d) <u>I</u> read the application form.
e) My <u>sister</u> works in a bank.

Q3 Here is an example of what you could write:

The computer course will start at 9 am and finish at 5 pm. There will be a lunch break at 1 pm and two coffee breaks. Bring a pen and a notebook with you.

Page 71

Q1 a) <u>T</u>he dentist only had an appointment for <u>F</u>riday<u>.</u>
b) My manager said <u>I</u> could take the day off<u>.</u>
c) <u>W</u>ho should <u>I</u> write a letter to<u>?</u>
d) <u>I</u> am going on holiday to <u>T</u>urkey<u>.</u>
e) <u>W</u>ould you like to join our tennis club<u>?</u>
f) <u>W</u>e want to go to <u>C</u>ornwall for our holiday<u>.</u>
g) <u>D</u>oes this train go directly from <u>P</u>ortsmouth to York<u>?</u>
h) <u>I</u> am going to the cinema with <u>A</u>nita tonight.

Page 75

Q1 a) past
b) present
c) future
d) present
e) future

Q2 a) writes
b) cooks
c) wash
d) were
e) are

Q3 a) I <u>bought</u> four tomatoes but they were rotten.
b) We <u>were</u> at football yesterday.
c) I <u>caught</u> the train, but I was still late.
d) You <u>are</u> going to go to the beach tomorrow.
e) They <u>went</u> to a meeting yesterday.

Page 77

Q1 a) The children <u>play</u> in the park.
b) The fire alarm <u>rings</u> on Tuesdays.
c) She <u>walks</u> to the shops every day.
d) I <u>throw</u> away the bananas.

Q2 a) I could <u>have</u> done it yesterday, but I forgot.
b) You should <u>have</u> come to the party.
c) They <u>have</u> done the shopping already.

Page 79

Q1 a) The college offers childcare courses <u>and</u> it organises work placements.
b) She was late for work <u>because</u> her alarm did not go off.
c) I want to buy a bike <u>so</u> I can get fit.
d) They went to the shop <u>but</u> it had already closed.
e) You should try this tea <u>because</u> it is lovely.
f) I will either wear the blue shoes <u>or</u> the pink shoes.
g) He built the cupboard carefully <u>but</u> it was still a bit wobbly.

h) At the park, we saw Ryan <u>and</u> he had his new dog with him.

Q2 Answers may vary, for example:
a) I am not feeling very well.
b) I can drive to work.
c) she did not like the old colour.
d) the sink has flooded.
e) I could go for a walk.
f) they were too short.
g) we can both come.
h) he could pay you back.

Section Five — Using Correct Spelling

Page 81

Q1 a) brief
b) weight
c) piece
d) neighbour
e) receive
f) field

Q2 Answers will vary, for example:
Because = <u>B</u>ig <u>E</u>lephants <u>C</u>an <u>A</u>lways <u>U</u>nderstand <u>S</u>mall <u>E</u>lephants.
Could = <u>C</u>ows <u>O</u>nly <u>U</u>se <u>L</u>arge <u>D</u>oors.
Weird = <u>W</u>ooden <u>E</u>lephants <u>I</u>n <u>R</u>ed <u>D</u>resses
Height = <u>H</u>appy <u>E</u>mily <u>I</u>s <u>G</u>etting <u>H</u>er <u>T</u>rain.

Page 83

Q1 a) book<u>s</u>
b) boy<u>s</u>
c) sandwich<u>es</u>
d) hal<u>ves</u>
e) countr<u>ies</u>
f) f<u>ee</u>t

Q2 a) The loa<u>ves</u> of bread I bought were too hard.
b) Can child<u>ren</u> eat at your restaurant?
c) We are making two new dish<u>es</u> today.
d) I talked about my hobb<u>ies</u> in the interview.

Page 85

Q1 a) disagree
b) careful
c) carried
d) having

Q2 a) I remembered the file as I was leav<u>ing</u>.
b) The instructions were <u>un</u>necessary.
c) She tr<u>ied</u> to phone the call centre again.

Page 87

Q1 a) Your order <u>may be</u> ready to send tomorrow.
b) You must have previous <u>experience</u> to apply.
c) We chose a <u>different</u> route to work today.
d) <u>Where</u> are you going for dinner?
e) <u>Thank you</u> so much for coming.
f) I <u>succeeded</u> in persuading him.
g) <u>Should</u> I drive the van?
h) We <u>wrote</u> out the report.

Q2 a) What
b) business
c) describe
d) whole
e) which
f) when
g) complaint

Page 91

Q1 a) to
b) been
c) teaching
d) Our
e) They're
f) your
g) brought
h) there

Q2 a) The driver did not see the bike <u>there</u>.
b) <u>Your</u> handbag is in the locker.
c) I did not <u>know</u> that the bank was open today.
d) <u>Our</u> flat is above the pub.
e) I have always wanted to work for <u>your</u> company.
f) Miriam <u>brought</u> cakes to the office.
g) I drove <u>too</u> close to the kerb.

Writing Test Practice

Each exam board gives a different length of time and a different number of marks for each writing task. Ask your teacher which exam board you are doing so you know what to expect in the real test.

You should aim for nine or more marks out of twelve to pass.

Exercise A (Page 94)

You should plan your writing and write a draft before you start your final answer.
(You can get up to 2 marks for planning and drafting your work.)

You should set your email out correctly:
- Start with 'Dear Madam' because you don't know the manager's name.
- Finish with a sign-off like 'Many thanks' because you don't know the manager. Then write your own name.
- Use paragraphs and full sentences. Start a new paragraph for each new point.

Your writing should:
- Be serious because you don't know the person you are writing to.
- Be polite because you want to make a good impression.

(You can get up to 2 marks for using the correct kind of writing for the person you are writing to.)

You should include this information:
- Why you are emailing her. You have seen her poster, and you would like to help out at the animal shelter.
- Why you would like to join her team. For example, you like animals and you want to help look after abandoned ones.
- Any skills you have which might be useful. For example, you are good at caring for animals, or you are a fast learner.
- When you are available to help. For example, every Saturday morning, or on Wednesday evenings.

Use a clear structure:

- Start by saying why you are emailing her. You are asking to volunteer at the shelter.
- Go on to say why you want to join her team, what relevant skills you have and when you are available.
- End with what you want her to do. For example, that you are looking forward to receiving her reply.

(You can get up to 4 marks for including the right information in a sensible order.)

You should use correct spelling, punctuation and grammar.

(You can get up to 4 marks for using correct spelling, punctuation and grammar.)

Exercise B (Page 95)

You should plan your writing and write a draft before you start your final answer.

(You can get up to 2 marks for planning and drafting your work.)

You should organise your writing:

- Use paragraphs and full sentences. Start a new paragraph for each new point.

Your writing should:

- Be serious because you don't know the person you are writing to.
- Be interesting to make the judges like it more than the other entries.

(You can get up to 2 marks for using the correct kind of writing for the person you are writing to.)

You should include this information:

- Where your house would be. For example, in the town you grew up in, or in Australia.
- What rooms it would have. For example, a cinema or a gym.
- What the garden would be like. For example, large with a pond or full of animals.
- Any other features it would have. For example, a swimming pool or four garages.

Use a clear structure:

- Start by saying where your house would be.
- Go on to give more details about the house
- End with something that sums up how good the house would be. For example, it would be the perfect house for anyone who likes cars.

(You can get up to 4 marks for including the right information in a sensible order.)

You should use correct spelling, punctuation and grammar.

(You can get up to 4 marks for using correct spelling, punctuation and grammar.)

Exercise C (Page 96)

You should plan your writing and write a draft before you start your final answer.

(You can get up to 2 marks for planning and drafting your work.)

You should set your letter out correctly.

- Start with 'Dear Sir or Madam' because you don't know the person you are writing to.
- End the letter with 'Yours faithfully' because you don't know the person's name. Then write your own name.
- Use paragraphs and full sentences. Start a new paragraph for each new point.

Your writing should:

- Be serious because you don't know the person you are writing to.

(You can get up to 2 marks for using the correct kind of writing for the person you are writing to.)

You should include this information:

- What the problem is. The question tells you that the cakes you bought from the supermarket were mouldy.
- When you bought the cakes. For example, 30th June.
- Where you bought them from. For example, their supermarket in Mifton.
- What you would like them to do about it. For example, refund the price of the cakes, or improve the quality of their cakes in the future.

Use a clear structure:

- Start by saying why you are writing the letter. You are complaining about some mouldy cakes.
- Go on to give information about when and where you bought them.
- End by saying what you want them to do about it.

(You can get up to 4 marks for including the right information in a sensible order.)

You should use correct spelling, punctuation and grammar.

(You can get up to 4 marks for using correct spelling, punctuation and grammar.)

Exercise D (Page 97)

You should plan your writing and write a draft before you start your final answer.

(You can get up to 2 marks for planning and drafting your work.)

You should organise your writing:

- Start your email with a friendly greeting like, 'Hi Wun Ling' because you are writing to someone you know.
- Use a friendly ending, for example, 'See you soon' and your name.
- Use paragraphs and full sentences. You should start a new paragraph for each point.

Your writing should:

- Be chatty and friendly because you are writing to someone you know. Don't use text language though.

(You can get up to 2 marks for using the correct kind of writing for the person you are writing to.)

You should include this information:

- Why you are emailing them. The question tells you that you are sending them some information to help them settle into your area.
- What they could do on the weekend. For example, go to the cinema or visit the nature reserve.
- Where they can park in the town centre. For example, there are two large car parks in the centre of town or there is always space to park on Dawson Road.
- Where to find useful places. For example, the Post Office is on Greenfield Terrace or the Bank is on Station Street.

(You can get up to 4 marks for including the right information in a sensible order.)

You should use correct spelling, punctuation and grammar.

(You can get up to 4 marks for using correct spelling, punctuation and grammar.)

Exercise E (Page 98)

You should plan your writing and write a draft before you start your final answer.

(You can get up to 2 marks for planning and drafting your work.)

You should set your personal statement out correctly:

- Use paragraphs and full sentences. Start a new paragraph for each new point.

Your writing should:

- Be serious because you don't know the person who will read your statement.

(You can get up to 2 marks for using the correct kind of writing for the person you are writing to.)

You should include this information:

- Why you would like to work at the bakery. For example, you like baking cakes or you would like to learn new skills.
- What experience you have. For example, you have worked in a shop before or you studied cookery at school.
- Any other information about yourself. For example, that you are hardworking, good at working in a team or you like to learn new things.

Use a clear structure:

- Start by saying why you are writing the statement. You're applying for the bakery assistant job.
- Go on to say why you want to work there, and why you think you would be good at it.
- End with a sentence that sums up why you think you should get the job.

(You can get up to 4 marks for including the right information in a sensible order.)

You should use correct spelling, punctuation and grammar.

(You can get up to 4 marks for using correct spelling, punctuation and grammar.)

Exercise F (Page 99)

You should plan your writing and write a draft before you start your final answer.

(You can get up to 2 marks for planning and drafting your work.)

You should organise your writing:

- Use paragraphs and full sentences. Start a new paragraph for each new point.

Your writing should:

- Be quite serious because you don't know the person you are writing to.
- Be quite friendly because you want her to buy your furniture.

(You can get up to 2 marks for using the correct kind of writing for the person you are writing to.)

You should include this information:

- What the sofa is like. For example, a cream leather sofa with only small marks, 2 years old.
- How much you would like to sell it for. For example, £200.
- Where you would like the sofa to be collected from. For example, the town centre or Grey Street.

(You can get up to 4 marks for including the right information in a sensible order.)

You should use correct spelling, punctuation and grammar.

(You can get up to 4 marks for using correct spelling, punctuation and grammar.)

Exercise G (Page 100)

You should plan your writing and write a draft before you start your final answer.

(You can get up to 2 marks for planning and drafting your work.)

You should organise your writing:

- Use a greeting like, 'Hello everyone' because you know the people you are emailing.
- Use a friendly sign-off like 'See you all soon' and your name.
- Use paragraphs and full sentences. Start a new paragraph for each new point.

Your writing should:

- Be chatty and friendly because you are writing to people you know. Don't use text language though.

(You can get up to 2 marks for using the correct kind of writing for the person you are writing to.)

You should include this information:

- When you would like to go on holiday. For example, next July or in about four months.
- Where you would like to go. For example, Crete or Prague.
- What you would like to do there. For example, go to the beach or do some sightseeing.
- When you would like them to reply by. For example, by the end of the week or as soon as possible.

Use a clear structure:

- Start by telling your friends that you would like them to come on holiday with you.
- Go on to describe the holiday and say why you want to go there.
- End with a sentence that asks them to reply so you can book the tickets.

(You can get up to 4 marks for including the right information in a sensible order.)

You should use correct spelling, punctuation and grammar.

(You can get up to 4 marks for using correct spelling, punctuation and grammar.)

Exercise H (Page 101)

You should plan your writing and write a draft before you start your final answer.

(You can get up to 2 marks for planning and drafting your work.)

You should organise your writing:

- Use paragraphs and full sentences. Start a new paragraph for each new point.

Your writing should:

- Be serious because you don't know the people you are writing to.

(You can get up to 2 marks for using the correct kind of writing for the person you are writing to.)

You should include this information:

- What you thought about the rooms. For example, they were very clean or they were cold.
- What the food was like. For example, the breakfast was delicious or the portions were too small.
- How the staff treated you. For example, everyone was very friendly or you could not find anyone when you had a problem.
- Whether you would stay there again.

Use a clear structure:

- Start by introducing yourself as a customer who stayed at the hotel last weekend.
- Go on to describe your stay, and what you thought about the hotel.
- End by giving your overall view of the hotel and whether you would stay there again.

(You can get up to 4 marks for including the right information in a sensible order.)

You should use correct spelling, punctuation and grammar.

(You can get up to 4 marks for using correct spelling, punctuation and grammar.)

Exercise I (Page 102)

You should plan your writing and write a draft before you start your final answer.

(You can get up to 2 marks for planning and drafting your work.)

You should organise your writing:

- Use paragraphs and full sentences. Start a new paragraph for each new point.

Your writing should:

- Be serious because you don't know the person you are writing to.

(You can get up to 2 marks for using the correct kind of writing for the person you are writing to.)

You should include this information:

- What you think of one of the suggestions so far. For example, you do not like the youth club idea because you think the building should be used for people of all ages, not just young people.
- What you think the building should be used for. For example, a community centre or a library.
- Why this would be good for the community. For example, it would be a place for people to socialise.

Use a clear structure:

- Start by talking about one of the suggestions given in the text.
- Go on to talk about your own suggestion.
- End by saying how the change will be good for the community.

(You can get up to 4 marks for including the right information in a sensible order.)

You should use correct spelling, punctuation and grammar.

(You can get up to 4 marks for using correct spelling, punctuation and grammar.)

Exercise J (Page 103)

You should plan your writing and write a draft before you start your final answer.

(You can get up to 2 marks for planning and drafting your work.)

You should organise your writing:

- Use paragraphs and full sentences. Start a new paragraph for each new point.

Your writing should:

- Be serious because you are writing to someone important (your line manager).

(You can get up to 2 marks for using the correct kind of writing for the person you are writing to.)

You should include this information:

- When and where the accident happened. For example, on Thursday afternoon in the workshop.
- What happened and how badly you were hurt. For example, you tripped over some boxes and twisted your ankle.
- Whether you will need time off work. For example, you will need a week off to recover.

Use a clear structure:

- Start by giving them information about when and where the accident took place.
- Go on to give details about what happened and how badly you were hurt.
- End by saying if you think you are able to work.

(You can get up to 4 marks for including the right information in a sensible order.)

You should use correct spelling, punctuation and grammar.

(You can get up to 4 marks for using correct spelling, punctuation and grammar.)

Exercise K (Page 104)

You should plan your writing and write a draft before you start your final answer.

(You can get up to 2 marks for planning and drafting your work.)

You should set your email out correctly:

- Start with a greeting like 'Dear Uncle Bob' because you know the person you are writing to.
- End with something friendly like 'Looking forward to seeing you' and your name.
- Use paragraphs and full sentences. Start a new paragraph for each new point.

Your writing should:

- Be chatty and friendly because you are writing to someone you know. Don't use text language though.

(You can get up to 2 marks for using the correct kind of writing for the person you are writing to.)

You should include this information:

- The date and time of the party. For example, Saturday 20th October at 8 pm.
- Where the party will be. For example, your parents' house or the Town Hall.
- What the party will be like. For example, fancy dress or an evening meal.
- Whether you need them to do anything. For example, bring a cake, invite other relatives, or keep it a secret.

Use a clear structure:

- Start by inviting them to the party.
- Go on to give them details about the party.
- End by saying whether you need them to do anything.

(You can get up to 4 marks for including the right information in a sensible order.)

You should use correct spelling, punctuation and grammar.

(You can get up to 4 marks for using correct spelling, punctuation and grammar.)

Exercise L (Page 105)

You should plan your writing and write a draft before you start your final answer.

(You can get up to 2 marks for planning and drafting your work.)

You should organise your writing:

- Use paragraphs and full sentences. Start a new paragraph for each new point.

Your writing should:

- Be serious because you don't know the people you are writing to.
- Give people lots of facts about the festival.

(You can get up to 2 marks for using the correct kind of writing for the person you are writing to.)

You should include this information:

- Where and when the festival will take place. For example, Eastfields park on 31st August.
- The type of music that will be playing. For example, rock, folk, pop or a mixture of styles.
- What other attractions there will be. For example, fair rides, games or food stalls.
- How people can buy tickets. For example, on the festival's website, in local shops or at the entrance to the festival.

(You can get up to 4 marks for including the right information in a sensible order.)

You should use correct spelling, punctuation and grammar.

(You can get up to 4 marks for using correct spelling, punctuation and grammar.)

Glossary

A

Article

A piece of writing in a newspaper or magazine.

B

Bullet points

A way of breaking up information into separate points in a list.

C

Controlled assessment

A part of the qualification that is taken during class time and marked by the teacher.

E

Email

A message sent over the internet.

F

Form

A text which is made up of questions with spaces for you to write your answers in.

Future tense

Writing that talks about something that will happen in the future.

G

Glossary

A part of a text which explains the meaning of difficult words.

Grammar

Rules that you follow so your writing makes sense. For example, you should write 'she makes' instead of 'she make'.

Greeting

A phrase used to start a letter or email. For example, 'Dear Mr Brockton' or 'Hello everyone'.

I

Instructions

A list of sentences that tell you how to do something.

J

Joining word

A word like 'and' or 'because' that joins parts of a sentence together.

K

Key words

The most important words in a sentence or a text. They tell you what the writing is mainly about.

L

Layout

How a text is presented on the page using things like subheadings and tables.

Leaflet

A text, which is usually given away for free, that tells the reader about something.

Letter

A text written to a person, or a group of people, which is sent in the post.

P

Paragraph

A group of sentences that are about the same thing.

Past tense

Writing that talks about something that has already happened.

Personal statement

A piece of writing about yourself, usually to apply for a job or a college course.

Prefixes

Letters added to the start of a word which change the word's meaning.

Present tense

Writing that talks about something that is happening now, or that happens all of the time.

Punctuation

Symbols which make your writing clearer. For example, full stops and capital letters.

R

Report

A text that gives the reader information about something. For example, an accident report.

S

Sign-off

A phrase used to end a letter or an email. For example, 'Yours faithfully' or 'Best wishes'.

Silent letters

Letters in a word which you can't hear when the word is said out loud. For example the letter 'k' in the word 'knew'.

Subheading

A title for one section of a text. A subheading usually says what the section is about.

Suffixes

Letters added to the end of a word which change the word's meaning.

T

Text

A piece of writing. For example a letter, a report or an email.

V

Verb

A doing or being word. For example 'run' or 'was'.

W

Web page

A type of text found on a website.

Index